Serving
with the Poor in
Africa

Tetsunao Yamamori, Bryant L. Myers, Kwame Bediako and Larry Reed, editors

A division of World Vision International
800 West Chestnut Avenue, Monrovia, California 91016-3198 USA

Other books in this series:
Serving with the Poor in Asia

Serving with the Poor in Africa
Tetsunao Yamamori, Bryant L. Myers, Kwame Bediako and Larry Reed, editors

ISBN 0-912552-98-0

Published by MARC, a division of World Vision International, 800 West Chestnut Avenue, Monrovia, California 91016, U.S.A.

Printed in the United States of America. Editor and interior page layout: Edna G. Valdez. Cover design: Richard Sears. Cover photo: Randy Miller.

Contents

Editors and contributors   v

Acknowledgments   ix

Introduction   1
Tetsunao Yamamori

Part One - Case Studies

1   From relief to development in Ethiopia   15
Mulugeta Abebe

2   AIDS awareness and challenge, Uganda   29
Mary Tyler

3   Resettling the pastoralists in Uganda   41
Hyeong Lyeol Lyu

4   Home care for AIDS patients in Zimbabwe   51
Kathy A. McCarty

5   Holistic lending by Zambuko Trust, Zimbabwe   67
Evans Maphenduka and Larry Reed

6   Rushinga cattle project in Zimbabwe   79
Denias B. Musona

7   Reaching the lost through community health in Ghana   93
John Oduro Boateng

8   Holistic ministry in large-scale relief, Mozambique   105
Tomas Valoi

Part Two - Reflections

9   Community participation and holistic development   123
Samuel J. Voorhies

10   A biblical framework for management practice   149
Kweku Hutchful

92458

11 Sociological and anthropological reflections   169
    Olivia N. Muchena

12 Theological reflections   181
    Kwame Bediako

13 Missiological reflections   193
    Roy Musasiwa

Part Three - Conclusion

14 At the end of the day   213
    Bryant L. Myers

Appendixes

A   Consultation participants   227

B   Case study guidelines   229

Editors and contributors

Tetsunao Yamamori (book co-editor and author of introductory chapter) is president of Food for the Hungry International. He served as steering committee chairman for the Harare consultation. He was professor and director of intercultural studies at Biola University and holds a Ph.D. in sociology of religion from Duke University. His published works are in missiology, sociology and international development.

Bryant L. Myers (book co-editor and author of concluding chapter) is vice president for strategy and Christian mission at World Vision International and is also director of MARC (Mission Advanced Research and Communication Center). He is a member of the Administrative Committee of the Lausanne Committee for World Evangelization and co-chair of Lausanne's Theology and Strategy Working Group. He has a Ph.D. from UCLA in biochemistry.

Kwame Bediako (book co-editor and author of chapter twelve) is a minister of the Presbyterian Church of Ghana. He holds doctorate degrees in French and Theology. He is also director of Akrofi-Cristaller Center for Mission Research and Applied Theology in Akropong-Akuapem, Ghana. He is visiting lecturer at the University of Edinburgh and a director of the Oxford Centre for Mission Studies at Oxford, England.

Larry Reed (book co-editor and co-author of chapter five) serves as the regional director for Africa and the Caribbean for Opportunity International and lives with his family in Harare, Zimbabwe. He has worked with Opportunity for eleven years and has contributed to many publications on the subject of microenterprise development. He holds a Master of Public Policy degree from the John F. Kennedy School of Government at Harvard University and is a graduate of Wheaton College.

Mulugeta Abebe (author of chapter one) has a Bachelor of Arts degree in Geography and a background in teaching. He has served universities and organizations in Ethiopia, Tanzania and elsewhere. In January 1995 he was appointed national director for World Vision Ethiopia.

Mary Tyler (author of chapter two) is a registered nurse, a midwife health visitor and a trainer in public health with many years of experience in the United Kingdom, Germany, Switzerland and Uganda. Since 1985 she has been in Uganda with Save the Children Fund/UK, seconded to Uganda's Ministry of Health, and with Food for the Hungry for the last five years working on the AIDS Awareness Project.

Hyeong Lyeol Lyu (author of chapter three) is an agriculturalist with Food for the Hungry, stationed in northern Uganda. A graduate of Seoul National University, he has served rural communities and churches in Korea assisted by his wife, Minja Lee, who is a nurse and midwife.

Kathy A. McCarty (author of chapter four) is a registered nurse with BSN and MSN degrees from the University of California, San Francisco. She serves as a minister of missions for Sebastopol Christian Church in California with an extended assignment at Chidamoyo Christian Hospital in Karoi, Zimbabwe, as clinical officer and matron.

Evans Maphenduka (co-author of chapter five) is the national director of Zambuko Trust, a microenterprise development organization based in Zimbabwe. He was formerly an accounting lecturer and chairman of the Accounting Department at the University of Zimbabwe. He holds a bachelor's degree in accounting and a master's degree in development finance from the University of Birmingham.

Denias B. Musona (author of chapter six) is the development coordinator for the United Baptist Church in Zimbabwe. He has worked with development projects in Zimbabwe for the past five years. He holds a diploma in biblical studies.

John Oduro Boateng (author of chapter seven) is a graduate of the University of Ghana Medical School and of the Haggai Institute in Singapore. He is national director of the Luke Society Missions in Ghana. Earlier positions include president medical doctor of Uniroyal Rubber Medical Center in Liberia and work with various mission hospitals in Ghana. He serves as an elder of the Church of Pentecost and on the board of Christian Health Assocation of Ghana and Sinapi Aba Trust.

Tomas Valoi (author of chapter eight) is the coordinator for World Vision Mozambique's Church Relation Project. A graduate of Maputo Commercial School, he previously served as senior commodities assistant within World Vision. He is a member of Union Baptist Church with the position of evangelist.

Samuel J. Voorhies (author of chapter nine) is a regional technical adviser for program and leadership development in the Africa

Regional Office of World Vision, Harare, Zimbabwe. Involved in holistic development ministry in 20 African nations over the last 15 years, he holds a doctorate in international development education from Florida State University. He is an adjunct professor at Fuller Theological Seminary, Pasadena, U.S.A., and the author of numerous articles.

Kweku Hutchful (author of chapter ten) is a native of Ghana and the founder of Leaders International. He travels as an independent consultant throughout the African continent on leadership development issues, conducting management training seminars for churches and Christian organizations, teaching in theological colleges, and advising on ministry and organizational development, human resource management and team building.

Olivia N. Muchena (author of chapter eleven) is the deputy minister of agriculture for the Government of Zimbabwe and the member of parliament for Mutoko South. Before that, she was a senior lecturer in the Department of Agricultural Economics and Extension at the University of Zimbabwe. She also serves with World Vision as the moderator of the World Vision Council, member of the World Vision International Board and chairperson of the Zimbabwe Advisory Board. She holds a Ph.D. in agricultural extension education from Iowa State University

Roy Musasiwa (author of chapter thirteen) is pastor of Calvary Baptist Church and academic dean of Domboshawa House Theological College since 1993 in Zimbabwe. He holds degrees from the University of Zimbabwe, the University of South Africa and Australian College of Theology. He is currently undertaking a Ph.D. in missiology through the University of South Africa. Previously he has held various positions including high school English teacher, general secretary of the Fellowship of Christian Unions and missions director for the Baptist Union of Zimbabwe.

Acknowledgements

In planning and executing a consultation, we must impose on a large number of people. To attempt to recognize them all is a sure way to inadvertently miss some. I want to thank, in advance, all those who have helped us in any way to bring about the success of this consultation. There are, however, people whom I must gratefully acknowledge by name. They are as follows:

Steering Committee members of the Africa Consultation: David Bussau (President, The Opportunity Foundation), Steve Ferguson (Senior Program Officer, Fieldstead & Company), Bryant Myers (Vice President for Strategy and Christian Mission, World Vision International), Don Stephens (President, Mercy Ships) and Cristina Houtz (Grants Administrator, Fieldstead & Company) who served as secretary of the Committee.

Africa Consultation Coordination: Coordinator Larry Reed (Africa Director of Opportunity International), Deputy Coordinator Cheryl Lovejoy and local preparation committee members (Sam Voorhies, Rose Gondo, Neill Mawhinney). As an able assistant to Larry, Cheryl expedited the entire preparation process of the consultation by issuing the call for case studies, arranging logistics and keeping track of expenses. She even assisted some case writers, unaccustomed to using English, in revising their papers. We owe a debt of gratitude to Cheryl.

Fieldstead & Company: Howard and Roberta Ahmanson for their unassuming role of encouragers and vision setters in funding the current series of holistic ministry investigations.

MARC: Bryant Myers and Jack Kenyon as director and publications director of MARC respectively for their ever-ready assistance and suggestions and for their competent supervision in producing a quality publication.

I should also mention and thank Amy McClain, my secretary at Food for the Hungry, who has shepherded the flow of communication between Harare and Scottsdale and between me and the members of the Steering Committee in addition to her already heavy load. Above all, I thank God for revealing to us the secrets of kingdom growth through these cases of effective holistic ministry cast in different contexts and circumstances.

Tetsunao Yamamori

Introduction

Tetsunao Yamamori

The Africa Consultation on Holistic Ministry was convened in Harare, Zimbabwe, in November 1995, with 30 representatives in attendance. *Serving with the Poor in Africa* resulted from the consultation and is a sequel to *Serving with the Poor in Asia*, published by MARC a year before. The format of the present volume is similar to that of the previous one. The case studies and reflection chapters constitute the main body of the book. The purpose of the consultation remains the same: to discover various models of development work that facilitate the formation of Christ groups. The authors of the case studies and the reflection chapters will inform and enrich the readers as to how people in various cultures come to know Christ while being helped to help themselves out of poverty.

The call for case study papers was sent out to various Christian agencies known to be involved in holistic ministry in all of Africa. The cases included in this book have met the criteria listed in Appendix B and the disproportionate representation of cases from Zimbabwe and Uganda is purely coincidental.

Further words on holistic ministry

In my introduction to *Serving with the Poor in Asia*, I stated: "A truly holistic ministry defines evangelism and social action as functionally separate, relationally inseparable and essential to the total ministry of the church. . . . Evangelism includes those efforts devoted to the proclamation of the Good News of God's salvation in Jesus Christ." Moreover, I have said that "social action encompasses those efforts devoted to the liberation of men and women from social, political and economic shackles." I now wish to expound further on the relationship between evangelism and social action from a biblical perspective. I would underscore the strategic importance of Christian relief and development in today's mission context.

Valson Thampu, an Indian scholar, delineates the main conceptual presuppositions of holism as follows: "(1) The whole is more than the sum of its parts, (2) the whole determines the nature of its parts, (3) parts cannot be understood if considered in isolation from the whole, and (4) the parts of an organic whole are dynamically interrelated or inter-dependent."[1] Holism, in other words, creates a synergistic effect and indeed the whole is more than the sum of its parts. The whole (namely, God's mission) determines the nature of the church's many missions. Holism implies the identity and distinctiveness of various parts in their relationship to the whole and, at the same time, their relationally inseparable nature. I consider Thampu's delineation very helpful in discussing the concept of holistic ministry.

Over the years there have been tendencies, in the name of holistic ministry, to emphasize one dimension of the church's concern (be it peace, social justice, poverty, human rights or the environment) to the exclusion of others and without connecting it to the mission of God. Books dealing with holistic ministry are often found wanting in their clear articulation of evangelism as being indispensable.

Holistic ministry to the whole person

The idea of holistic ministry has deep biblical roots. Throughout the Old and New Testaments, the Bible mandates that the church minister to the whole person. This means addressing both physical and spiritual needs through approaches that are inseparably linked but functionally separate. We see this idea in the three distinct forms of ministry common in the Old Testament roles of judge, prophet and priest.

The unique and complementary ministries of Moses and Aaron, for example, were fused together to buttress Israel's total life as God's covenant community. Moses delivered God's mandates and prophetic messages to the people. Aaron was a shepherd who helped people obey God's laws. These two functionally separate ministries were inextricably linked. Individual obedience to God's laws (delivered by Moses) depended on a spiritual desire to please God (taught by Aaron). Samuel's holistic ministry assumed all three distinct roles of judge, prophet and priest. Each of these offices was functionally separate, but all were necessary to strengthen and enrich Israel's community life.

The idea of holistic ministry is also evident in the prophets' lives and teachings. They directed men and women to pay attention both to their vertical relationship with God and their horizontal ties to each other. Hosea described the vertical relationship as "knowledge of God" and advocated its pursuit. Isaiah called on Israel to fulfill the horizontal relationship: "Seek justice, encourage the oppressed. Defend the cause of the fatherless, plead the case of the widow" (Isaiah 1:17).

Though the vertical and horizontal relationships are separate and different, the Old Testament teaching exemplified through Moses, Aaron, Samuel and the prophets clearly demonstrates that neither relationship can flourish without the other.

The New Testament also affirms the holistic ministry concept. Jesus' ministry embodied the idea of welding evangelism with social action. The apostle Paul's teaching and the life of the early church continued the theme.

Matthew 4:23 says that "Jesus went throughout Galilee, teaching in their synagogues, preaching the good news of the kingdom, and healing every disease and sickness among the people." Though teaching, preaching and healing were separate functions, they were all essential to the total ministry of Jesus. This is the case today with the body of Christ—the church.

In Romans and Ephesians, Paul says that this body consists of diverse members, each with his or her own function, all working together as a single unit. "Just as each of us has one body with many members, and these members do not all have the same function, so in Christ we who are many form one body, and each member belongs to all the others" (Romans 12:4, 5). Paul reiterates this theme in Ephesians 4:11-13, writing, "It was [God] who gave some to be apostles, some to be prophets, some to be evangelists, some to be pastors and teachers, to prepare God's people for works of service, so that the body of Christ may be built up until we all reach unity in the faith and in the knowledge of the Son of God and become mature, attaining to the whole measure of the fullness of Christ."

The chronicles of the first century church recorded in Acts show that the early Christians understood and lived out the notion of holistic ministry. They were engaged both in proclaiming the good news (evangelism) and in meeting each others' needs (social action). This strategy helped the church grow to one out of every 360 persons in the known world by the end of the first century.[2]

The role of missions and compassionate ministries such as those undertaken by Christian relief and development agencies today is becoming more urgent as the twentieth century draws to a close. Research shows that by the century's end, nearly a quarter of the world's population (1.25 billion people) will be completely unevangelized for Christ, with most of them living in closed or restricted countries.[3]

Further research indicates that Islam is the world's fastest growing religion. Analysts expect that today's Muslim population of one billion will double by 2020 and will grow from 19% of the world's population to 25%.[4] Today, about 33% of the world's population is Christian. This is expected to grow to only 35% by 2020.[5] Followers of Allah outnumber Christian believers of all denominations except Catholicism.[6]

Clearly we have made only slow progress in meeting our challenge to "make disciples of all nations." This is partly because of the high birth rate common to Third World countries, many of which restrict traditional missionary approaches. It is also because we have inadequately integrated the concepts of strategic timing and strategic placement of resources in our missions programs.

Strategic timing

To improve our strategic timing, George Otis, Jr. has developed the idea of spiritual mapping. This is a process of pinpointing and preparing for strategic windows of evangelistic opportunity. The idea is to place less importance on manmade boundaries (countries, economies and religions) and more on the spiritual significance of everyday events. According to Otis, "superimposing our understanding of forces and events in the spiritual domain onto places and circumstances in the material world" often results in borders, capitals and battlefronts different from their manmade counterparts.[7]

Applying spiritual mapping to the challenges of world evangelism can prepare evangelists to respond quickly and appropriately to spiritual windows of opportunity. The 1991 Gulf War and the fall of communism in Eastern Europe opened two such windows.

According to David Barrett, a handful of evangelical churches in Iraq and Saudi Arabia have experienced rapid growth as a result of the Gulf War. Some converts to Christianity are Arab.[8] At least a portion of this growth can be attributed to Christians worshiping openly while stationed on Arab soil during the war. These Christians responded to a strategic window of opportunity. Unfortunately, this is an all-too-rare occurrence in the church's history. We must think strategically about how to take advantage of future windows of opportunity before they are slammed shut.

One important key is rethinking the investments of our mission resources. In a 1988 *Together* article, Bryant Myers attempted to pinpoint the most strategic areas of the world to place mission resources. He wrote, "The poor are the lost and the lost are the poor . . . those who are the poorest and in greatest need of hearing the name of Jesus are living in the midst of Muslim and Marxist contexts in the Two-Thirds World."[9]

Dan Harrison sounded a similar theme in his book, *Hope for the World*, in 1991. He described a strategic geographic area for missions located between the tenth and fortieth latitudes. This area has come to be referred to as the "10/40 window," and it represents "great physical as well as spiritual poverty."[10]

Not only does the 10/40 window house more than 80% of the world's poorest people, it is also home to 90% of unreached people groups. Moreover, this area contains most of the countries that are closed to traditional missionary approaches. It is headquarters to nearly all non-Christian spiritual belief systems. It is a place of political and religious repression. Islam dominates the area. Conversion to Christianity can invoke the penalty of persecution, torture and execution.

The writings of Otis, Myers and Harrison all point to the 10/40 window as one of the most strategic geographic areas for deploying missionary resources. Yet while 90% of the world's unreached people groups live in the 10/40 window, this area merited only 3% of total missionary forces in 1990 and only .01% of average Christian family income.[11] As David Barrett and Todd Johnson have stated, in our missionary labors we continue to direct 96% of all our evangelizing activities at other Christians. This must be changed, and Christian relief and development agencies are in a unique position to effect such a change. A big reason for the skewed distribution of missionary resources is that traditional missionaries are often not allowed into the 10/40 window countries. But Christian relief and development agencies often can get inside because of the special skills and material aid they bring. Through these agencies, the church can successfully fulfill a biblical commitment to holistic evangelism and social action in the world's most strategic area. Accomplishing this requires understanding what I call "population types" and designing ministry strategies accordingly.

Targeting population types

In a Christian missions context, there are two kinds of populations: those that are open to Christianity and those that are not. I will discuss the two corresponding approaches to reaching these populations later. For now, I will differentiate the two population groups by using four indices: hospitality, evangelization, receptivity and development need.

Hospitality refers to the degree to which a country, social group or people group welcomes Christianity. It especially refers to the quantity and quality of social sanctions placed on gospel witness. Ninety percent of the world's unreached people groups live in countries with social or government policies prohibiting the entrance of missionaries and limiting or forbidding the evangelistic activities of national Christians.

Evangelization refers to the number of people within a population who have heard the good news of Jesus Christ and the degree to which they have received the message.

Receptivity gauges the degree to which individuals within a particular people group are open to the gospel. This differs from hospitality, which refers to societal or governmental limitations, not to the people's openness. For example, while the hospitality of China to Christian missions is low, the receptivity of the people is very high.

Development measures the physical condition of the target group. Peter McPherson, formerly of USAID, tells us that 90% of the world's population in the year 2000 will live in developing countries. Already, 75% of the world's population lives in the Third World. This means that more people than ever will experience some kind of acute physical need in the years to come. Obviously, the role of Christian relief and development is becoming more strategic to the church's total mission.

Using these four indices as a guide, we can classify population groups into two types: top-end and bottom-end. The top-end group is made up of countries or people groups that are most hospitable to Christianity, most evangelized, most receptive to the gospel and most developed. The bottom-end group consists of countries or people groups that are least hospitable to Christianity, least evangelized, least receptive to the gospel and least developed. The bottom-end population type is found to the greatest degree in the 10/40 window. Obviously there are countries and people groups that fall between these two extremes, but research is key to identifying accurately who they are and into which group they fall.

Strategic options

To effectively reach top-end and bottom-end population groups, "contextual holism" is necessary. This is a holistic ministry strategy that takes into account the needs, problems, opportunities, receptivity and available resources of a particular area to determine which aspect of holistic ministry should be underscored at any given time to fully accomplish God's work. The principle of contextual holism is sensible, practical, necessary and most important, biblical.

In the New Testament, Jesus determined the nature and type of his ministry in accordance with contextual factors. He engaged primarily in preaching and theological discourses when ministering to members of the upper classes such as Sadducees, Pharisees, lawyers and scribes. His work with the masses, on the other hand, included not only preaching and teaching but also healing and feeding. And in still other contexts, his ministry primarily was one of healing. In all these cases, the nature of the needs and the audience were factors determining his emphasis. In sending forth the twelve into a preaching and healing mission, described in Matthew 10, Jesus instructed the disciples that the nature of the people's receptivity to them should guide their movements.

The principle of contextual holism also determined the character of the early church's thrust and priorities. In the immediate aftermath of Pentecost, the church carried out its ministry in terms of preaching, teaching, healing and sharing, as illustrated in the book of Acts. As long as the church remained predominantly Jewish, it expressed its faith and life largely in the traditional Jewish context and continued such practices as worshipping in the temple and practicing circumcision. When the church moved into the Gentile world, the new context called for different expressions of faith and life, as is well known in Paul's strategy with the Gentiles.

Keeping in mind the principle of contextual holism, we see that a "harvesting" strategy is applicable to the top-end populations, while a "preparatory" strategy is relevant for the bottom-end populations.

Harvesting approach

The harvesting approach is a direct, traditional missionary strategy characterized by sharing the Word of God overtly and forthrightly. It is a common strategy where missionaries are welcomed and the people are openly receptive to the gospel. Many national Christians can be found in an area appropriate for the harvesting approach. Physical needs will not be so great that they overwhelm all other concerns.

The rapid growth of non-Christian religions among top-end populations makes it imperative that the church deploy missionaries with sound training in mission strategy and accurate knowledge of how people in different cultures become Christians. Many will need to specialize in responding to rapid urbanization and the growth of Eastern religions.

Preparatory approach

The preparatory approach is the strategy best suited for the 10/40 region and other countries at the lower end of the population scale. This approach involves doing something now in the hope that people will respond to the gospel later. It is appropriate in areas where career missionaries are not permitted to enter or the people are not yet responsive to the gospel. Typically, few or no Christians live in these areas. The people often need food, basic health care, education, information on proper nutrition, appropriate technology, food production and other things. In this setting, the development of one-on-one friendships can be the best strategy for leading nonbelievers to Christ. The ministry of Christian relief and development is well suited to this context. Workers in these agencies can "let [their] light shine before men" so that non-Christians will "see [their] good deeds and praise your Father in heaven" (Matthew 5:16).

A Food for the Hungry volunteer working within the 10/40 window recently reported attending a meeting to help a village articulate its agricultural needs. A few minutes into the meeting, a woman said, "If you want to know what we really need, we have evil spirits." A man retorted, "He knows only of agriculture. He knows nothing of evil spirits." The Food for the Hungry volunteer answered, "It so happens that I serve a living God that demons are afraid of." Over the next several months, the volunteer continued sharing his faith on a one-on-one basis in this highly restricted country. The number of conversions has not been as large as it might be in a harvesting context, but each conversion is no less dramatic. As villagers share with each other and leaders are trained in discipleship, the Christian movement within this village will become strong. To a large degree, this is because one woman saw the light of Jesus shining in one Christian relief and development worker. And that worker was ready to share his faith when the Lord provided an opportunity.

Preparing the soil

The preparatory strategy requires a different kind of missionary than the more typical harvesting strategy. Skilled relief and development workers who are guided by their "missionary heart" are best suited for the preparatory strategy. They can come from developed and developing countries. But a high degree of selectivity in staffing is critical. All Christian relief and development agencies have limited budgets. Host nations often place further limits on us by holding down the number of "expatriate" staff allowed into the country. This is especially true in closed or restricted countries. In light of such constraints, it is imperative to carefully select and meticulously train every expatriate relief and development worker. Moreover, great care should be taken in selecting national staff, since they are the best prospects for disciples who can continue the evangelism after the development team leaves.

Fulfilling the Great Commission

Christian relief and development organizations are in a unique position to help the church meet the challenge put before us in the Great Commission (Matthew 28:19-20). We must meet today's mission context with a strategy that recognizes the new dynamics surrounding us. This strategy must allow us to use our resources to penetrate areas of the world that are controlled by poverty, repression and spiritual deprivation. It must give individuals the means to lift themselves out of poverty—both physical and spiritual. Holistic ministry is such a strategy.

NOTES

1   Valson Thampu, *Rediscovering Mission: Towards A Non-Western Missiological Paradigm* (New Delhi: Theological Research and Communication Institute, 1995), p. 4.

2   Thomas Wang, ed., *AD 2000 and Beyond*, Vol. 1, No. 5 (November-December 1990).

3   David Barrett and Todd Johnson, *Our Globe and How to Reach It* (Birmingham: New Hope, 1990), p. 25.

4   Reported on ABC's "Nightline," February 15, 1989.

5   Conversation with David Barrett, Southern Baptist Convention Foreign Mission Board, September 17, 1991.

6   David Barrett, ed., *World Christian Encyclopedia* (New York: Oxford University Press, 1982), p. 777.

7   George Otis, Jr., *The Last of the Giants* (Tarreytown: Fleming H. Revell Co., 1991), p. 87.

8   Conversation with David Barrett, April 23, 1992.

9   Bryant L. Myers, "Where Are the Poor and the Lost?" in *Together* (October-December 1988).

10 Dan Harrison, *Hope for the World* (Downers Grove: InterVarsity Press, 1991), p. 49.

11 Barrett and Johnson, pp. 25-27.

Part one

Case Studies

1

From relief to development in Ethiopia

Mulugeta Abebe

Worl Vision International has been ministering to the needy in Ethiopia since 1971. With the establishment of a field office in 1975, the organization has conducted extensive development and child care projects in the country. The massive relief aid and rehabilitation programs that World Vision Ethiopia (WVE) conducted in Ethiopia between 1984 and 1989 helped save the lives of millions. The Ansokia I ADP (area development program) readily depicts the multidimensional aspects of the organization's relief and development work.

This case demonstrates how Ansokia I has extended its ministry from relief operations to an integrated rural development scheme that is based on multifaceted participatory intervention. I will attempt to show the reader how these principles, objectives and goals were implemented at Ansokia I ADP. I will welcome your comments, suggestions and recommendations.

Case study context

History of the Ansokia community

Ansokia I ADP is located 350 kilometers north of Addis Ababa. The area lies within the watershed of one of Ethiopia's largest rivers—Awash and the Borkena river basin. Makoy, the administrative center of Ansokia district, is connected by a 12 kilometer all-weather road to the main road, constructed with WVE support.

The program covers 18 peasant associations (PAs), with a total area of 18,995 hectares and a population of 45,000 people, comprising 7,586 households. The average annual population growth is 2.9%; the average family size is 5.4 persons. There are two major people groups living in Ansokia I: Amhara (70%) and Oromo (30%). The main religions are the Coptic Orthodox church and Islam.

Most of Ansokia's community members engage in mixed farming and animal husbandry. Nonfarming activities are primarily limited to blacksmithing, pottery, basketmaking and petty trading. Of the 18,995 hectares, 7,918 hectares (42%) are under cultivation, 3,039 (16%) are used for grazing and the remaining 42% is uncultivated. The livestock raised are cattle, sheep, goats and poultry. Crops grown in the area include teff, maize and sorghum in the lowlands and midlands, while barley, wheat and pulses are grown in the highlands. Other agricultural activities include beekeeping, coffee cultivation and horticultural farming.

Existing social services include two junior secondary schools, seven elementary schools, three clinics and six health spots. The nearest referral hospital is at Dessie, 32 kilometers north of the project area.

Some 20 years ago, the hills and mountains adjacent to the Ansokia valley were covered with dense natural forests. With the high population growth, the demand for arable land and grazing area increased. People began to clear forests on steep slope areas that are unsuitable for cultivation. As a result, serious deforestation and land degradation occurred. The area began to experience recurrent drought, which significantly reduced crop production and the community's economy. By the early eighties, Ansokia had turned into a dust bowl.

The 1984 drought that claimed the lives of many Ethiopians also seriously affected the Ansokia community. During that time, Ansokia's inhabitants lived in untold destitution. People were deprived of basic needs such as food, shelter, clothing and medication.

The area was cut off from the main road and, due to the prevalence of malnutrition, an average of 15-20 people were dying daily. Potable water, intervillage communications and educational facilities were uncommon in the area. Community members remained ignorant of the Word of God.

In October 1984, WVE began its program in the area through relief operations to save the lives of the drought victims by establishing two feeding camps.

Culture of the community

The Ansokia community is traditionally organized into family groups and structurally lives in subvillages (locally known as *got*, comprising an average of 100 household heads). Three to four subvillages form one village, locally known as a Peasant Association (PA), comprising 300-400 family heads.

At the subvillage level the community has traditionally elected elders who serve as administrators. In addition to the traditional community leaders, there are PA council members elected by the community through local government authorities. These council members are responsible for all political, social and economic matters of the community. The local religious leaders play a role in guiding and advising community leaders.

The villagers empower the elders to take full responsibility in decisionmaking and the settlement of disputes by using traditional bylaws. Community members have strong cultural links that enable them to live in harmony. They also have traditional forms of mutual self-help organizations, whereby community members assist each other by sharing ideas, resources and labor.

Respect for the elders and the senior members of the community has been an important cultural element, and WVE has properly employed this in its operations in Ansokia. Joint decisions passed by the community elders and WVE facilitators were implemented accordingly.

Coptic Orthodoxy and Islam are religions practiced by the vast majority of the population. The many religious holidays observed by the peasants and the festivals associated with these holidays remained a counterproductive practice that had a negative impact on grassroots development. Belief in fate and other traditional values and the people's negative attitude toward manual labor—represented by artisans, weavers and tanners—hampered the development of appropriate technology. This is true mainly of the Orthodox believers. Muslims practice long fasting seasons (Ramadan), which drastically reduces their ability to be productive during such times.

Description of the holistic ministry program

Development approach

WVE believes that development goals can be achieved when the community fully participates at all levels of the development process. WVE's community based technical program (CBTP), one of the tools used to initiate the ADP approach, ensures the community's direct involvement in all programs. This has enabled the people to become self-reliant goal owners of their development endeavor.

The CBTP approach is designed to enhance participation through facilitation techniques and incorporating program development skills to bring attitudinal and behavioral changes among community members. The approach emphasizes team building, integration of sectoral activities, program development, on-the-job training, skill transfer and participation.

The community's involvement was encouraged as early as 1986. In the same year, WVE made an extensive evaluation of various projects that were conducted in the rural areas of the country. This gave birth to the CBTP concept. Further, design plans were prepared for five projects, one of which was Ansokia I.

To emphasize the sustainability of ongoing development programs in the area, various committees were established to monitor and manage the community development activities, such as agricultural extension and conservation, health, water development, child development, gender development and flour mill management. These committees are elected by community members to ensure grassroots participation. In each of these communities, elected members also learn how to manage their activities with the assistance given to them by WVE technical personnel.

There was no local church in the area that had the desire to make contact with WVE. The establishment of an evangelical church in Ansokia was initiated in the process of the development of the ADPs and the evangelization of the area. At first, the Muslim population was either indifferent to or ignorant of the whole situation. The Orthodox churches were not ready to entertain such goals.

Program interventions

The relief operation was launched by establishing a feeding center, which also provided health services. The relief food aid was given in the form of intensive wet feeding (for those who were on the verge of death), supplementary and dry feeding.

A total of 4,683 metric tons of grain and over 40,000 pieces of clothing were distributed to over 68,000 drought victims. The implementation of the relief program was instrumental in forging a viable relationship between WVE and the community.

With the culmination of the relief program in 1987, a rehabilitation program was launched to ensure stability among community members. This was followed by a brainstorming and evaluation session. The participatory evaluation of the relief and rehabilitation programs enabled WVE staff to come up with a long-term integrated and sustainable development approach.

Further reformulation of the CBTP approach gave rise to the development of the Ansokia I ADP design plan. In 1990 the ADP system, based on a participatory comprehensive development program, came to surface at Ansokia I. Before these activities, WVE conducted an extensive base line survey at Ansokia, consulting with local government officials and line departments on the mode of the implementation of development programs in various areas of rural development.

It was in the rehabilitation phase that Ansokia I ADP started sponsoring children. In 1988, a total of 2,165 children in six peasant associations were enrolled. In 1995, the number of sponsored children grew to 8,768.

The main features of the Ansokia I ADP intervention program included capturing local resources, environmental rehabilitation, access to social services, wider area and community coverage and effective resource mobilization. Construction of bridges, roads, vocational training, agriculture, afforestation, soil conservation, beekeeping, water development and evangelism were some of the activities during this phase. This was also a period in which WVE was able to integrate past experience with new and challenging tasks.

WVE learned lessons from its relief and rehabilitation programs and continued promoting its program through the ADP approach. It has learned that a community-centered integrated development program and local resource tapping leads to sustainability, while free handouts result in dependency. The combined effort has improved the lives of the poor through the full participation of the community members and implementation of the designed programs.

Major interventions of the Ansokia I ADP are:

1. Agricultural extension dealing with input distribution (oxen, cows, goats, sheep, beehives, poultry), livestock upgrading, training of staff members and farmers.
2. Afforestation and soil conservation through provision of seedlings to farmers, establishment of individual and community-owned satellite nurseries, training of farmers, physical and vegetative conservation measures.
3. Gender and development: Vocational training skill transfer, introduction of income generation activities, provision of inputs such as sewing machine, cows, goats and vegetable seeds, introduction of energy-saving mud stove and better home management.
4. Health: Focus on community participation and behavioral and attitudinal changes through continuous consultation and training, family planning and AIDS prevention.
5. Infrastructure: Construction and maintenance of roads, schools, clinics and health posts, maintenance of feeder roads, digging of water points, introduction of appropriate

technologies such as mud stoves, mud bricks and modern beehives.

Results and impacts of the program

1. Participation and empowerment: The ADP has fostered the creation and development of local self-management, such as sectoral development committees. For example, community members are now more aware of their problems and their environment. They are in a position to take initiatives in mobilizing their labor and locally available resources to implement integrated development programs. Their capacity to adopt new innovations, such as improved home management, environmental sanitation, crop diversification, afforestation and soil conservation has been enhanced.

2. Economic and social gains: There is growing community interest in various innovations introduced by WVE. These include improvements in crop production and diversification, bio-intensive gardening, agroforestry, woodlot plantation, fuel-efficient mud stoves and beekeeping. Some specific examples are:

    a. Crop production: Provision of improved tools, seeds, and techniques made available to individual farmers have resulted in an increase in yield per hectare. Changes in the project area as a whole show that the average yield of 800 kilograms has increased to 1,200 kilograms per hectare. Provision of oxen through the credit scheme enabled the community members to plough their fields and plant in a timely manner. The total area under cultivation also increased from 7,980 hectares to 8,218 hectares. Vegetable production, which did not exist before the introduction of the ADP, is now a significant contributor to the diet and is a cash crop in 15 peasant associations.

    b. Biointensive gardening practices: Farm communities now have cash income from the sale of produce. Ato Mulu Argaw, from Mekdessa Aroressa PA, earned approximately US$260 in 1994 from a total plot area of

1,554 square meters. He allocated the extra income for food, clothing, the purchase of goats and savings.

c. Agroforestry: Many farmers now practice intensive agroforestry farming on their small plots for profit. Abate Abrha from Atko Godguade PA and Ahmed Tsegaw of Mekdessa Addis Amba PA planted fruit trees, including orange, papaya, mango, gishta, guava, as well as coffee and sugar cane on their plots. Ato Abate Abraha, who started agroforestry quite recently, received a good profit last year from the first harvest of papaya, orange and coffee. He has allocated the income toward the purchase of onion seeds to generate further income. Ato Ahmed Tsegaw received almost US$700 in gross income from his agroforestry activities on a plot of 6,400 square meters. The income was generated from 125 papaya plants and 1,789 sugar cane plants. He has allocated most of this money for iron sheet roofing for his house, and the rest for farm activities and household consumption.

d. Woodlots: You cannot find a farmer in Ansokia who did not plant trees around his house. Ato Tsegaye Bekele, for example, planted 2,500 seedlings of eucalyptus and of these, he sold 400 and made approximately US$255, while using another 400 trees for house construction and energy. He spent the money on clothes and medication and was able to put most of the money into savings.

e. Fuel-efficient mud stoves: Beneficiaries confirmed that it has helped them save energy, time and money. In a sampling of seven households with an average family size of five, the newly-introduced stove has reduced the bundles of wood they use for energy from 122 to 40. As a result, more time and energy has been given to development programs.

f. Improved beehives: The average yield from the traditional type is 6 kilograms per beehive, while the yield from the improved beehives is 18 kilograms. The planting and maintaining of biointensive gardens and agroforestry plots have also had a positive effect in the yield increase. Ato Abebe Beyene, who used to harvest 3 kilograms of honey per season from two traditional beehives, is now getting 14 kilograms from one improved beehive.

The construction of health facilities and the supply of adequate and safe water for drinking have improved the overall health of the community. Because of the construction of school buildings, the provision of classroom equipment and the sponsorship program, school enrollment has increased by 25 percent.

Today many farmers in the area are self-sufficient in food production. Surplus production is bringing more cash to fill gaps in their financial needs. The major effects related to food security include an increase in average yield per hectare by 50% and total cereal crop production by 56% in the 18 PAs of the ADP. The total increase of productive land is 4% (300 hectares), and the diversification of agricultural production has been accomplished with the introduction of new cereal crops, biointensive gardening and agroforestry.

Ansokia, otherwise known as the "dust bowl" of the 1984-85 drought in Ethiopia, has been a focal point for several approaches to food production. Despite its record in 1984-85, when an estimated 20 people a day were dying as a result of drought-induced famine, no relief undertakings have been recorded for the area since then.

Christian witness

Evangelism

Ansokia I's Christian witness activities and their impact date back to the program's formation. The exemplary lives of the staff members attracted many people from the community to come to Jesus. The Christian love exhibited by Ansokia staff, especially during the 1984-85 drought, touched the hearts of the children and adults and led them to accept Jesus Christ as their personal Savior and Lord.

The survivors of the cruel famine could not forget the ministry done in their midst. What WVE staff did in saving people from physical death, in nursing the sick and in helping to bury the dead planted unforgettable memories in the minds of the residents of Ansokia.

23

"This special commitment and Christian love has helped to draw many Muslims and nonbelievers to the kingdom of God," recalled the ADP manager. In the absence of a Christian church in the area, the task of Christian nurturing was mainly conducted by WVE staff. Measurable development impacts through the program and discussions the staff conducted with individual community members contributed to the intensity of Christian witnessing.

With the growing number of new believers in the area, WVE sent an evangelism enhancer to facilitate the nurturing of new believers. When teaching the basics of the Bible to new converts became a necessity, WVE invited various denominations to come to the area and involve themselves in the Lord's ministry within the Ansokia community. In 1988 an evangelical church was established in Ansokia. Today this church has over 700 members and 100 children attending services and Sunday school.

The Ansokia church has two full-time evangelists, as well as church elders and deacons who actively participate in the dissemination of the gospel and the enhancement of grassroots development. One of the evangelists worked in the Ansokia I ADP for about seven years and the other evangelist was a former beneficiary of WVE's relief operations in the area. In each village of the ADP there are church fellowship cells that gather together for worship. Regular evening prayer meetings are conducted twice a week. These meetings and cells became excellent forums for the enhancement of the ideas of holistic ministry to the inhabitants of Ansokia I.

The establishment and strengthening of an evangelical church in Ansokia I is the product of the consolidation of Christian witness that dates back to the period of famine relief and rehabilitation. WVE staff members exploited the opportunity to teach the Word of God in the feeding centers. The growth in the number of those who accepted Jesus as their Savior led to the establishment of Christian fellowship groups that later developed into a new church. Now the church has a day care center that also teaches the Bible to the younger generation in Ansokia. The church also works in close collaboration with Ansokia I ADP.

"Ansokia I ADP is promoting these activities even beyond its project areas. It has stretched out to Macaw (to the north 325 kilometers), to Ataye (south 75 kilometers), up to Ajibar (west 180 kilometers), and up to Dubti (east 300 kilometers)," said Ato Wondimu Feleke. "We address all churches through training, special courses, Bible provision, tracts and visits, and we provide them with available copies of the Holy Bible."

The experience of Ansokia I ADP shows that the existence of a dynamic and growing church and Christian community is an indispensable factor for sustainable transformational development. Thus Ansokia I is supporting local churches by providing them with leadership training, and organizing conferences and meetings with the local churches.

Interviews

Ketema Bekele, 30, lives in Ansokia. He is well aware of the changes that were introduced in the area as a result of WVE's evangelistic activities. He tells his story as follows:

"I had never heard of Jesus before. But I was suffering from severe nose bleeding and migraine headaches. After I survived the famine through WVE's assistance in the wet feeding center, I went to WVE's health staff to ask for medication. Ato Ayuele Dubale, one of the medical staff, said, 'Get up, for how long are you going to be depressed and without hope? You are not relieved. What shall we do?'

"I said, 'I have no idea, please tell me what I should do!' He said, 'If you believe in him, Jesus can heal you.' I allowed him to pray for me and finally the evil spirit was cast out of me and all my sickness was gone for good. Since then I have been a follower of Jesus. I am bringing many people to Christ, too."

Another story is that of Aynalem Yiman, who told us, "The money is ours, the work is ours, the responsibility is ours." He is the Ansokia I ADP committee chairman. Here are more excerpts from his comments: "I resisted the call of Jesus through many WVE staff for more than ten times. However, I was involved in the development work. Their accountability and dedication to the spiritual and physical work touched my heart. I watched them praying and talking about the ways in which they can bring about a better life for us. I finally gave up last year and received Jesus. Since then, I have shared the joy, the responsibility and the work that WVE staff shared with us. I now understand why WVE staff have been struggling for the improvement in our standard of living.

"I have observed that dedicated Christianity brings good accountability. In various ADP committees, the Muslims and others are nominating the born-again Christians to be the treasurers of their flour mills, water development, revolving loan scheme and other committees. This shows that Christ makes the difference in the lives of people."

Evaluation and conclusion

From our experience in Ansokia I ADP, we have been able to prove that our approach to rural development was timely and appropriate. As a result of WVE's intervention in Ansokia, the rural poor gained from the primary health care programs, agricultural improvement packages and rural infrastructural facilities. Ansokia, a rural community of the hungry and poor, was turned into a green and fertile area inhabited by industrious farmers. Famine in Ansokia became a thing of the past, unknown to children who were born in the area since 1983.

Ansokia I actually became a demonstration center on how a community-based technical program could become a solution to underdevelopment through community participatory interventions. Ansokia I also showed that small-scale integrated intervention covering wider areas could bring effective results in rural transformation. Further, by way of expanding our efforts in reaching unreached areas, attempts should be made to build the capacity to live up to our expectations. Much has been done, but despite the successes some challenges are still ahead.

The prevalence of cultural conservatism had a role in determining the pace of development and the spiritual transformation of the entire community. Nonetheless, promoting the managerial capacity of community members and their full involvement in community activities needs more attention and training. Drought and the periodic reappearance of malaria were some of the major obstacles to be tackled in Ansokia. With the establishment of the ADP these problems were solved. Now the process of the internalization of rural development ideas needs to be enhanced. Also, the role of women in development is improving but the challenge of breaking the cultural attitude that disfavors women has not been eradicated. And special attention should be paid to focusing on small-scale enterprise endeavors.

The people of Ansokia had been living in extreme poverty for ages. We cannot expect to solve all their problems in a decade. Still, there is more to be desired. For Ansokia I, the future appears bright but there is still more to be accomplished.

2
AIDS awareness and challenge, Uganda

Mary Tyler

The communities on the outskirts of Kampala, Uganda, are generally rural, and only a few encroach on the suburbs of the city. The primary means of income generation are agriculture and small trade. The area has been recovering from a period of social instability, which ended in 1986 with the present government. Though peace and economic development have prevailed in the country as a whole, the rural population has been unable to make equal strides forward due to, among other things, AIDS. The communities have been destabilized because of the destruction of traditional authority structures, including the family, during twenty years of civil unrest. The result has been a massive spread of AIDS.

There has been one regime since 1986, which has been benevolent and under which peace has prevailed. Economic development has occurred under this government, with the economy improving since 1986. A constitution that includes elections is being discussed, further providing a sense of hope for the future. Many of the rural population have not been able to make many improvements, however, because much of the manpower is dying of AIDS and because many of their resources are being used on expensive cultural customs such as weddings and funerals. This, in turn, continues to drain money from other key areas, such as education. Many hope to see their children educated in the university and thus place a high priority on money for school fees. But these fees are more difficult to secure in the present environment and many of these hopes go unfulfilled.

Communities are experiencing greater peace and less fear in their daily lives as they recover from a long period of insecurity. However, the civil unrest has taken its toll. Much of the adult population in the communities were killed during that time and the result has been a generation ignorant of traditional values and God's law. They have lived "loose" lives and have thus promoted the spread of AIDS. The loss of the adult members of the community has also reduced the number of wage earners and has decreased agricultural output and associated income. The standard of living has greatly decreased during the last 20 years.

Even in the midst of these problems the communities continue to be very supportive of one another. This mutual support is strengthened by their poverty. Families assist others with weddings, funeral and educational expenses as a kind of investment toward the same provision in the future when the time arises. Life increasingly revolves around death and death rituals. No family is untouched by AIDS, so all are involved with someone who is sick and dying from AIDS, and someone for whom they have had to arrange a funeral. But even this sense of family and community is under strain. Extended families find their resources further stretched as they take in the increasing numbers of AIDS orphans.

The two main religious forces in these communities are the Protestant and Catholic churches. There is a high church attendance rate in comparison with Western standards. Most of the participants, however, see church as a way to earn God's pleasure rather than as a means of encouraging a personal faith and walk with God. This is also true of many of those who are baptized as infants but no longer attend services. Interestingly enough, there is a high perception among people as to whether they are saved or not.

Christianity is making a difference, however, among families affected by AIDS. In many families where there is no commitment to Christ, frequent divorce or multiple spouses unsettle the children (in some cases children have been turned out), and make them feel unloved. Many of these youth turn to their peers or to rich benefactors who give them some sense of being wanted, but it is usually at a high cost of exposure to AIDS.

Description of our project

Our project addresses the lack of care for AIDS patients and their families, and the sexual promiscuity that promotes the spread of AIDS. The project is built on a number of community strengths in relation to AIDS. For example, the communities desire to do something to express love to the AIDS patients and their families. But in the past they have not been sure how to do so, and due to the day-to-day necessities for survival they have been unable to set aside time to make plans. Another strength is the influence the Church of Uganda has in the communities. Yet a third strength is the presence of existing churches, which have served as forums through which mobilized people could be trained and organized to act on their training.

Technically, our project is considered a health project with a focus on AIDS prevention and improving the care of AIDS patients, as well as addressing the psychological needs of their families. The project began when an expatriate and a Ugandan pastor sat down to pray and ask God what he would have them do about the destruction caused by AIDS. They decided to work through the Sunday morning church services and other existing church structures such as choirs, youth groups and Sunday schools. In each of these contexts they would discuss the problem of AIDS through music, drama, overhead projections and exposition of the Bible.

The first service begun under this program was attended unexpectedly by the wife of the president of Uganda, who added her support by expounding on 2 Chronicles 7:14: "If my people, who are called by my name, will humble themselves and pray and seek my face and turn from their wicked ways, then will I hear from heaven and will forgive their sin and will heal their land." This was followed by a play called *Why Me?* which depicted the impact of

AIDS on family life. Many people were moved to dedicate themselves to change during this service.

Food for the Hungry International (FHI) then entered into a partnership with a Church of Uganda diocese. FHI's program was twofold: 1) approach donors with an AIDS prevention proposal called "Youth Challenge" for the Church of Uganda parish youth groups, and 2) start a ministry to AIDS patients and their families through the Church's leadership to secure cooperation in implementing the project in the parishes. Pastors were organized to produce a discussion manual that focused on the dangers of AIDS and what youth needed to do to avoid these dangers. The slogan, "Leap to a Healthier Lifestyle," was established with an appropriate emblem that was printed on T-shirts. Any young person committing to this new lifestyle was taught how to lead a discussion group by using questions to stimulate thought. In Sunday morning services in each parish, the AIDS team would give an AIDS awareness presentation.

The first step in the development process was to secure the cooperation of the diocesan bishop, and get his support in introducing the program to one of the archdeaconries under him. With the bishop's support, FHI project staff then introduced the program to the chosen archdeacon. With the archdeacon's support, an "Introductory Day" was held with pastors and other leaders of churches in the archdeaconry, to secure their cooperation and set up a plan of action.

Following this initial interaction, these leaders and others they recommend are trained by FHI staff in the presentation of the "Challenge of AIDS" to their own parishes, assisted by FHI staff. The FHI staff then worked with each parish to prepare music and drama that would support the AIDS awareness information and the biblical message presented in the Sunday morning "AIDS Challenge Service." In the service, the youth are asked to get involved in the church youth group and begin using the discussion manual developed by the pastors to address the problem of AIDS and what they can do about it.

At another service, called the "Good Samaritan Service," a challenge is given to the members to get involved in serving AIDS patients and their families, who are socially ostracized. After this an "Implementation Training Day" is held in a specific parish to train leaders and others interested in how to effectively lead the youth group discussions, and how to stimulate care for the sick among church members. The parishes then carry on these programs on their own with occasional follow-up visits by FHI staff.

Critical assumptions in the project are as follows:

1. A changed lifestyle is fundamental to defeat AIDS.
2. Commitment to Jesus as Lord changes lifestyles, which defeats AIDS, and allows people to go beyond meeting basic needs to fulfill their God-given potential.
3. God answers prayer.
4. God has called us to be involved in the work under his will.
5. People attend church for cultural rather than religious reasons.
6. Culturally adapted communications will result in a greater knowledge of God's Word and a better understanding of how to deal with AIDS, and music and drama are effective ways to communicate in this culture.
7. AIDS can be conquered as people respond to God's call to repentance.
8. Existing church institutions and structures are a good foundation on which to build the program, and will lead to a greater possibility of sustainable impact.

The key principles we followed in our program include:

1. Conform all teaching and training to the Word of God and never compromise.
2. Pray "without ceasing" for the program and beneficiaries, listening to that "still, small voice," and be convinced that God answers prayer.
3. Implementers should be fully committed to the Lord and the program.
4. Identify the key innovators in a community or church who live a Christ-centered life, and mobilize them to commit to the program.

5. Respond to the church's or community's own identified needs—not to the implementer's ideas.
6. Conduct ongoing review with objectives in mind, and seek to avoid dependency.

The local church was involved in the program from its inception. The program began with a pastor and a FHI staff person who shared a burden to do something about the AIDS epidemic. The program has continued to seek the church leadership's cooperation. A primary goal is to use and build on existing church structures and institutions, primarily through training. The church is the primary implementer (e.g., the music and drama are presented by church members and not by FHI staff) of this program, with FHI serving primarily as facilitator and trainer.

FHI staff and the church's pastor issue a challenge to the congregation at the presentation during the Sunday service to come forward and accept Christ as their Savior, who will also help to guide them through the problems AIDS presents. The lives of the youth also act as a witness to their peers as they demonstrate the fruit of the Spirit (primarily self-control), and the joy associated with walking with Christ. The older members of the congregation show the love of Christ by visiting ostracized members of their community and bringing with them gifts of love, showing a desire to listen to problems and praying for them.

Results of the program

One of the most significant results is that AIDS patients began to experience love and affection, rather than ostracism. In one parish alone, after mobilization the number of patients visited increased from 45 to 170 per month. Family members of AIDS patients, after experiencing a compassionate visit, have become involved in the Good Samaritan committee themselves. Visiting Good Samaritans take small gifts (sugar, tea, salt, soap and clothing) to patients to make them a little more comfortable.

These Good Samaritan committee members were frustrated before FHI's involvement, because they saw a need but did not really know how to go about helping the sick. After being challenged and trained in how to visit, they have eagerly gone out to minister the love of Christ. They share their enthusiasm in the work with others, and the membership of one committee has increased from 10 to 40 members. They report that the AIDS patients and their families are much more willing to have them visit, thereby making their work more enjoyable. In one church, monthly cash contributions to the committee's work amounted to about US$6. This amount increased to US$10, and one income generating project produced an additional US$30 for the committee's use. This does not include the food and clothing brought for the committee's use. Committee members benefit from the mutual support and encouragement of the weekly meetings, where needs are identified and the use of resources is discussed.

The following improvements have been seen in the lives of the poor as a result of the program:

1. Those who were visited no longer feel ostracized by their community.
2. Committed youth who practice a changed lifestyle are protected from AIDS and other sexually transmitted diseases, as well as from physical abuse. They also have lifestyles that avoid drug addiction.
3. Sick people are getting much-needed food items, such as sugar and tea.
4. Churches have developed their own income-generating projects to help their poor members.
5. Individuals have seen the value of income-generating projects and have embarked on other non-church related areas such as a farmers' association to help improve the farmers' income.

The following are indicators of spiritual change as a result of the program:

1. During the challenges to accept Christ as Savior given at the AIDS awareness services over the past three years, 891 people have come forward.
2. Visiting Good Samaritans have shared the gospel with patients on their deathbeds. In one parish 30 dying people

and seven family members have accepted Christ as their Savior.

3. At a "Fun Day" organized to help youth better occupy their spare time, a challenge was given and 12 accepted Christ as Savior.

4. At a training program for church leaders the challenge was given and 23 accepted Christ as Savior.

5. Attendance in Sunday morning services have increased (in one case going from 500 to 1,000), church membership has increased, the number of children in Sunday school has increased, youth group membership has increased and attendance at various other church groups has increased.

6. In one active parish the Good Samaritan team has motivated the parish to devote itself to pray every day at 10 P.M. for the sick, the poor and others in need.

7. Family members of AIDS patients, after experiencing a compassionate visit, have begun attending church.

8. In one parish two young men in wheelchairs who could not attend church are now being brought to church by caring members.

Evidence of cultural and social change as a result of the program:

1. In Uganda many couples live together without formal marriage. They know a church wedding is a commitment and they do not want to make it. But this program has resulted in couples deciding to sanctify their marriages in the church and commit to each other.

2. Parents and church leaders exposed to training in this program are now asking for education in topics that were once considered taboo.

3. People who are dying from AIDS were once ostracized by their communities, but now community members are visiting them and making them feel the love of Christ in their last hours.

4. Parents are having more of an impact in the education (especially sex education) of their children. This was confirmed by

responses to a question asked during an evaluation of the program.

5. Youth are spending less time in discos and other places where they are exposed to contacts that promote the spread of AIDS. They are spending more time in healthier activities such as sports, reading and helping others. This was also documented by evaluation results.

6. More people are taking an active interest in their community and the needs of its members. For example, one young man has volunteered to teach in school wearing the T-shirt that identifies him as a person committed to a healthier lifestyle.

The process of people coming to know Christ

The method with the most easily visible results is the challenge given during awareness services. A purposeful attempt is made to show the need for Christ in one's life during the service, and then a call is made at the service's close. Those who come forward are met by the team and the church leaders after the service, and counselled about growth and the need to continue fellowship in the church.

Training of the church's music and drama groups is organized so that the group's presentation either shows a clear need for Christ in one's life or clearly offers a challenge to the congregation to accept Christ. As mentioned above, church members challenged to visit the sick are trained in visitation, including how to share their faith with the people they visit. In this way a number of people have come to Christ, but how many have been reached by this method is unknown.

Another of the methods used is that prior to special events such as a "Fun Day", the organizers are trained so that sometime during the event a need for Christ is presented, and a challenge is given. During training of the church leadership in preparation for launching the program in a parish, the details of AIDS and its implications are presented along with the challenge to accept Christ as one's Savior.

One of the key individuals in the program is the project manager. The project manager coordinates with church leaders and key people to secure cooperation and data needed for program. She or he is also responsible to see that the project maintains a biblical focus. Another key individual is the music and drama coordinator, who trains the choir and other church participants for the service and sometimes gives the challenge. Both the youth coordinator and the home care coordinator play key roles in the program by participating in the services and training.

Evaluation of the case

The following are the improvements I would make to the program:

1. Focus on small work areas and on families.
2. Involve the program with Sunday school and primary school children that are part of the identified parish. The youth are the most vulnerable and are influenced most by what they learn from peers and in school.
3. Keep a low profile in the church and community, and be very sensitive to the impact of external visitors on patients.
4. Maintain prayer without ceasing, and listen to God.
5. Work with the pastors and church leaders who catch the vision; they will in turn influence their churches and communities.

The following are the obstacles we encountered in the course of our work:

1. The pastors' workloads and social habits increasingly revolve around death and funerals. As deaths increase, they find little time to do anything else. Their focus is on the urgent or immediate need.
2. Rain: Many social activities come to a halt during rains and rainy season.
3. Traditional cultural habits that prevent change, although these are decreasing as education expands.
4. The traditional church's hierarchy has been very slow to respond to the challenge of AIDS.
5. Major donor policy that focuses on condom distribution,

which promotes promiscuity and confuses the youth when they are presented with the message of celibacy.

6. The attitude that money solves all problems, and that Uganda deserves outside help to solve its problems.

3
Resettling the pastoralists in Uganda

Hyeong Lyeol Lyu

The rural community located in the Mbarara District in south-west Uganda was established by the government when it gave land from a portion of a national game park to people who used to live in mid-Uganda but were displaced by conflict. The Mbarara District has a population of 929,600 according to the 1991 census, which is the most recent.

This relocation produced a community with no traditional authority structures or natural cohesion. Since it used to be a game park, wild animals roam the area and seem to favor crops over wild plants as their primary food source. Grazing plants and rain are critically important to these pastoralists. The allocated land is not adequate to meet cattle needs during the dry season, and families migrate frequently in search of pasture and water for their animals.

The area is ruled by a man personally appointed by the president who feels he only answers to the president, and who has taken personal credit for any advances made in terms of infrastructure development. He has said that the people are incapable of managing anything themselves, but he does not take any action to develop their skills. Besides AIDS orphans, this community's sacrifice during the civil war has produced many war orphans.

This group of people suffered more than others because they directly supported President Museveni when he was a rebel. Since he was from their area, he hid in their communities. The government then in power knew that they were harboring Museveni, and so attacked and ransacked villages where they thought he was. The government also attacked and killed people suspected of sympathizing with and supporting the rebels. Many witnessed the death of loved ones, had their homes and property stolen or destroyed and had their most important material possession, their cattle, taken from them. Since these communities supported and sequestered Museveni's rebel activities, they feel he is in debt to them. They believe they should be provided for rather than expected to sacrifice and provide for themselves.

The community is very open to religion, and many baptized as infants feel they are Christians, but they have stopped going to church for various reasons. Some have decided doing business on Sunday is more important; others have sin in their lives and so feel unworthy to attend church services. Some were offended by a church member in the past, and some feel they do not get anything out of church.

Poverty causes the people to work together in dealing with the significant events in their lives. Families support other families in wedding, funeral and education expenses so they can expect the same support when their time of need arises.

Most people are so busy dealing with today's problems that they have little time, energy or ability to plan for future needs. They still feel a strong desire to reach out to others, but cannot plan how to do so. They are happier when someone gives them a plan to help them deal better with the problems they see around them.

As we began our work in this community and assessed the needs that were to be addressed, we found that the people were not accustomed to farming, neither were they motivated to farm. In the former game reserve, wild animals roamed the area, destroying the crops that the people attempted to raise. The people also lacked a basic understanding of the meaning of a relationship with Christ, its impact on their day-to-day lives and their support of the church.

Finally, poverty was so serious that people could not afford to educate their children or support the educational system.

One of the community strengths upon which we were able to build was that the people have a strong willingness to share. When anyone in the community has a need, people willingly contribute to the need by sharing their own resources. This is especially true for important events, such as weddings and funerals. Another strength is that there is a good amount of land available to the community members on which to build their agricultural efforts.

Economically, these people suffered greatly in supporting the current president's rise to power in 1986. Most lost homes, cattle, many assets and family members. They were moved to the present area and promised many benefits that have been very slow in coming. Their traditional base of economy—the cow—does poorly on the small piece of land they have been given. They are of the royal part of their tribe, and as such do not feel they should "dig" (i.e., farm), so to train them to become farmers requires a major shift in their world view. Both pastors and teachers have found it difficult to work full-time at their jobs because of inadequate incomes.

Socially, the communities are living on land allocated to them, so the traditional lines of authority have been obliterated. People are not related to their neighbors as they were in traditional communities. New leaders are slowly emerging from the new community, but these tend to be the high-profile, well-educated people rather than those in place in a traditional community.

Politically, the community is a resettlement community, and thus falls under the authority and care of the government's Ministry of Labour and Social Welfare. This ministry appoints a person over this resettlement scheme, who is responsible to the ministry for developments on the scheme. The first few appointees did not work out for various reasons, so the president himself stepped in and appointed a person directly from the Presidential Secretariat. This appointee was known to the president because he was previously a school teacher of the president's. He was also of the same tribal group as the people of the resettlement community, although from a different part of Uganda. These factors probably contributed to his being chosen for this particular community. Since this person represents the community to the government he wields considerable power, which can and has been abused.

Religiously, the community is primarily Protestant. Few manifest a personal relationship with Christ, nor do they practice biblical standards of responsibility. In addition, church attendance is low because the people see little value in going to church. Pastors have historically found it very difficult to serve full-time because of the poor income the church has provided.

Description of our program

This is an agricultural program focusing on training and motivating people to practice agriculture. Training events are arranged so that the whole person is addressed, and includes materials on salvation, spiritual maturity, health and education.

The project began in November 1992 when the government invited Food for the Hungry International (FHI) to get involved with the development of the people in this resettlement area. In response, FHI's expatriate project manager, Mr. Lyu, moved into the area with his family.

A study had revealed that income generation could be increased if people planted their own banana gardens. Bananas are a staple of the local diet, so with their own gardens people could feed themselves, and market the extra produce for increased income to meet other needs.

Farmer support was enlisted to begin planting bananas. Farming implements were given to interested individuals and schools because they were pastoralists and had none. Those who showed an interest by preparing an area for planting and opening a path for a vehicle to bring the plants were given about 50 banana shoots. Since these people needed to care for their animals while being motivated to farm, FHI staff decided to encourage the digging of rainwater reservoirs to meet their needs for water and keep them from wandering away from the area in search of water. FHI staff also encouraged the planting of other crops, such as beans, sweet potatoes and cabbages, but it was found that unless the gardens were protected, the wild animals would eat them. So farmers were provided with barbed wire (free at first, later at subsidized rates) to protect their gardens.

As some farmers began to prosper and develop confidence in our approach, more people wanted to begin farming. As demand increased, training programs were planned that not only taught people how to farm better, but also showed them their need of Christ, the need to practice hygienic living, the need to immunize their children, how to raise healthier animals and the need to be involved in and improve education. In time farmers were taught to share (tithe) their produce with the church and with their neighbors; sharing banana shoots to encourage other farmers to start gardens proved quite a success.

Later, FHI staff worked with church leaders, discipling them and encouraging them to reach out to their neighbors through personal visits. This has improved the sense of community and increased church involvement. Last, FHI focused on developing the ability of schools to be self-sustaining by encouraging the planting of gardens, from which the produce could be used as food for the students or sold to assist with expenses.

The critical assumptions made during the course of the work are:

1. Changed lifestyles are fundamental to defeat poverty.
2. Commitment to Jesus as Lord changes lifestyles, which defeats poverty and allows people to go beyond meeting basic needs to fulfill their God-given potential.
3. God answers prayer.
4. God has called us to be involved in the work under his will.
5. People attend church for cultural rather than religious reasons. If we define "religious" as seeking to worship and improve a personal relationship with God through Jesus, this is not the reason people attend church. What people do is gather to express solidarity with others who have been baptized into the same denomination, and to ensure that when their time of need comes for a "religious" function such as a funeral or wedding, they will get reciprocal support. Religion has become a series of cultural habits and norms.

6. Poverty can be conquered as people respond to God's call to change their lifestyle.
7. To make an impact on a community, it is important to build good relationships with the leaders and the people.
8. Create opportunities for meeting people to share the love of God with them.
9. Create opportunities for discussions that help people to see their God-given potential.

The key principles we followed were:

1. The development worker has to be *with the people* and try to bear their problems with them, and walk with them in seeking God's will in solving those problems. Mr. Lyu, the Korean expatriate agriculturalist and project manager, built a house in the resettlement community among the people. He went out daily in his work as an agricultural adviser, spending time with the community members in their fields and in their homes. He developed relationships with people, which he nurtured by contact during non-work or recreational hours. He worshiped with them in their churches. He and his family lived among them, and so he was with the people.
2. Training beneficiaries to transfer ideas to one another creates a greater impact.
3. A development worker needs to be a listener.
4. We must work to see what the people bring to solve their own problems.
5. Cooperating with other NGOs and government officials creates a greater impact.

The church was involved with the program from the project's initial introduction to the community. This involvement took the form of acting as translators between the people and the development workers. This raised the status of the church in the community's eyes. Church leaders were included in home visitation teams to teach them the value of home visitation in the church's own development.

In terms of Christian witness, the project staff shared their faith frequently with farmers as they visited them at their farms and homes. They also encouraged school teachers and people they felt were sensitive to the need to visit neighbors and share with them. This also led to sharing their burdens physically by digging in their gardens. Project staff also organized the showing of the Jesus film and the training of church leaders in spiritual ministry.

Results of the program

The results described below were gathered through a baseline survey completed when Mr. Lyu moved into the project area and through a more thorough evaluation completed at the start of 1995. Since Mr. Lyu lived and worshiped with the people, he was able to constantly monitor the progress they were making and he knew the condition of their religious activities.

Of the 530 families in the resettlement area, 400 now have their own gardens and can feed their families without outside assistance. Two hundred of these families can pay for certain expenses, such as school fees for their children.

Of those with their own gardens, 97 have now protected them with barbed wire fencing. Three hundred farmers have shared their produce with either their neighbors or with the church. There are now nine water reservoirs in the area, all of which were constructed with an average of 70 percent inputs from the farmers themselves. Three schools and two pastors now have their own income-generating gardens.

Of the 500 families that raise cattle, 350 can meet cattle needs near their homes and do not have to uproot families and take children out of school in search of water and pasture. Although the government representative of the area at first said the people were unable to manage any kind of project by themselves, the people have now organized their own school and community development committees to discuss improvements they want to see undertaken, showing their growing sense of being a community.

In the two and-a-half years that FHI has been in service in the community, over 490 people have accepted Christ as their Savior. These people came to Christ on an individual basis and were from all sectors of the community—old, young, orphans, married people. During home visitations, 45 families renewed their commitment to Christ, repenting of ungodly behavior and deciding to be faithful to the Word of God. Before FHI began work in the resettlement area, church attendance at the Church of Uganda congregation was about 20 people on a regular Sunday. There are now about 200 people attending services every Sunday. At the Full Gospel Church the attendance has grown from 20 to 60 each Sunday. To date over 170 farmers have shared their produce with the church. They also opened six Full Gospel and nine Church of Uganda subparishes to handle the increased membership.

Process of people coming to know Christ

One method used to introduce people to Christ was to show the Jesus film, then issue a challenge to people to accept Christ as their Savior. Another method was personal sharing with people during visits to their homes and gardens by FHI staff.

The project manager worked with Life Ministry and with church, community and government leaders to organize the presentation of the Jesus film. He also organized and conducted training for church leaders on their responsibilities and how to evangelize and disciple people. He mobilized pastors and other church leaders to accompany him on home visitation trips, through which the church leaders could express care for and share their faith with community members. And he personally visited farmers to see the progress of their gardens, and to discuss problems and improvements as well as their own walk with Christ. The project manager also used his own resources to help build two churches in the community.

The church benefitted from the development program. Church gardens were promoted to improve support of the local pastors. Produce from the gardens were shared with the needy in their distress. The gardens also served as a type of extension farm to promote farming among all community members. The church leadership was trained in development practices, and discipled themselves. Discipleship and member-care was modeled for church leaders by FHI staff. It is hoped that the church will remain the primary force for development after FHI has left the area.

Evaluation of the program

The project manager lists several improvements he would make to the program:

1. Reduce the number of handouts that have added to the sense of dependency among the people.
2. Spend more time earlier in the program trying to mobilize the people to have a sense of ownership of the interventions, so that better use would be made of them and equipment or tools would not get "lost."
3. Reduce the number of people to work with, seeking to have a greater impact on fewer people who would then become the ones who promote development in the community, instead of depending on the project manager.
4. Be slower to use a vehicle among the people, which creates an attitude that the project manager is wealthy and capable of giving many things away.

The obstacles we encountered along the way were as follows:

1. A government-appointed director, who felt the people were incapable of managing themselves and only deserved handouts.
2. Government officers who had their own agenda for development among the people.
3. An attitude among the people that they had sacrificed enough for the government and now it was time for the government to pay them back with handouts.
4. An attitude among the people that they should not "dig," because they were of the royal class of pastoralists.
5. Roaming wild animals that devoured crops and destroyed gardens.
6. Drought, which killed some crops and set back development in the area.

4

Home care for
AIDS patients in Zimbabwe

Kathy A. McCarty

AIDS in Africa is an enormously encompassing problem reaching into all areas of the physical, social, psychological and spiritual environments of people. The response of the church in Africa to the AIDS crisis seemed to be one of complacency at first. Many felt this was a social problem that did not affect the church, so the church needed to stay out of it because this was God's plan to punish these sinners. This directly opposes the ministry of Jesus Christ. Jesus told the Pharisees: "It is not the healthy who need a doctor, but the sick. . . . For I have not come to call the righteous, but sinners" (Matthew 9:12-13).

The church is in a unique position to confront the AIDS situation. We have the Good News in a situation that has no good news from a medical or political standpoint. God has called us as a church to do the following things:

> *The Spirit of the Sovereign Lord is on me, because the Lord has anointed me to preach good news to the poor. He has sent me to bind up the brokenhearted, to proclaim freedom for the captives and release from darkness for the prisoners, to proclaim the year of the Lord's favor and the day of vengeance of our God, to comfort all who mourn, and to provide for those who grieve in Zion—to bestow on them a*

crown of beauty instead of ashes, the oil of gladness instead of mourning, and a garment of praise instead of a spirit of despair (Isaiah 61:1-3).

Africa, a continent with 9% of the world's population, contains 80% of the world's HIV-positive citizens. It is estimated that there will be 70 million Africans who will be HIV-positive by the year 2015. In some African countries, one-third of the population is infected. The cumulative total of reported AIDS cases in Zimbabwe reached 41,298 by the end of March 1995. One million Zimbabweans will die of AIDS by the year 2000. In all provinces and the major cities, there is a continued rapid escalation of HIV-related diseases.

As Christians and as organizations providing care in Africa we can face a crisis that will affect all of us and our work. AIDS is in the world and AIDS is in the church. Some of the first people to die from AIDS were Christian leaders in our area.

Case study context

Economically Zimbabwe is better off than most developing countries. People can have land in communal areas and most grow enough food for their families and have excess to sell in good rainy years. There have been two recent droughts in Zimbabwe (1991-92 and 1994-95), which have created difficult economic times for the people.

Politically, Zimbabwe has been stable since April 1980, when independence and majority rule were established. The country's first black African ruler, Robert Mugabe, was elected into power as prime minister. Mugabe has been reelected three times since and continues to rule a Socialist government with some leanings toward a free, capitalistic nation. In religious terms, Zimbabwe is Christian. Although most people profess a belief in God, a mixture of both ancestral worship and Christianity is common. Mission hospitals provide more than 60 percent of the rural health care services in Zimbabwe, having established most of the rural health care centers before independence.

Chidamoyo Christian Hospital is located in northwest Zimbabwe in Hurungwe District, a communal land where people are farmers growing maize, cotton, sunflower and tobacco crops for cash and for subsistence. Hurungwe District has a population of 265,000 people. Included in this area is the small farming town of Karoi and several commercial farms, as well as large communal farming areas.

The hospital serves a patient population of approximately 31,000 in the immediate 30 kilometer radius, and acts as a referral center for other clinics in the area. It is also the nearest hospital for people in parts of the Kariba and Gokwe Districts.

Chidamoyo Christian Hospital was established in 1968 as an evangelistic effort of the Churches of Christ in Zimbabwe. The purpose of the hospital was to holistically treat people with medical and spiritual needs. Many times this purpose was not in the forefront as the overwhelming need for medical care became more and more time consuming. Many times the staff had to reevaluate this ministry and get priorities in order. In 1991 the hospital experienced the beginning of the AIDS crisis with bed overcrowding, families unable to cope with the long hospitalizations and staff unable to cope with the demands of an ever increasing number of terminally ill patients and their families.

Shona culture prizes the family very highly, starting with the local family, then the extended family and on to people of the same totem (people who believe they have the same original father, and come from the same original area in Zimbabwe). This develops into a sense of community and of always belonging to a community.

Illness is not an individual problem, but a community problem. When people are ill they return to their rural homes to be cared for by their extended family. The people believe that witchcraft causes illness. Someone has bewitched you so that you are now ill, or because you have not done something to appease your ancestral spirits, which are now angry and cause illness or bad things to happen to you or your family. When a person is ill the family will go to great lengths and expense to find out the cause or person causing the bewitching by consulting n'angas (witch doctors). Doing what the n'anga instructs is thought to bring the eventual healing of the affected person.

53

This belief in witchcraft is widespread throughout Zimbabwe and in many African cultures. Urban Zimbabweans may see scientific reasons for diseases, but when affected by diseases that do not seem to respond to modern medicine many revert to consulting *n'angas*, often because of pressure from relatives and in the hope of receiving healing.

Many Christians still hold firmly to their traditional beliefs and fit them into their Christianity. They may go to church on Sunday and go to the *n'anga* on Monday without seeing any inconsistency in the practice. When faced with a life-threatening disease like AIDS, many Christians will try the *n'angas* in case it might work. Family members will put pressure on the individual to try and find out who is causing the illness.

Chidamoyo Christian Hospital decided to implement a program in response to the AIDS crisis. The program would deal with the crisis as a family problem and use the community as the primary care givers—supported by the medical community—instead of having institutionalized care for terminally ill patients. Using the strong family and community bond in Shona society, we were able to draw on these strengths to deal with the overwhelming disaster that AIDS was causing in the families and communities in Zimbabwe. Incorporated from the beginning of the project was the desire to minister holistically through medical, psychological, social and spiritual support of a person infected with AIDS and that person's family. AIDS is a disease of the family as well as of the community.

In 1991 the medical staff of Chidamoyo Christian Hospital began to feel the need to expand from hospital care of patients with AIDS to a holistic care, within their own community, of patients and families with AIDS. Realizing that medically the hospital did not have much to offer the patients, the staff decided to expand beyond the hospital into the community. With input from medical and chaplain staff at the hospital, a purpose statement and goals for the program were developed (see appendix at end of chapter). The purpose of this program was to be an integrated part of the hospital AIDS program, offering holistic care to patients and families affected by AIDS, and extending care into the community.

The holistic ministry program

The program started in April 1991 with a home care team consisting of one nurse and one chaplain. This team was to be an integrated part of the hospital care of the AIDS patient. From admission through discharge this team would see the patients every day. The nurse would plan the patient's medical care in the hospital until their discharge, while the chaplain would evaluate spiritual needs and follow-up upon discharge.

HIV infection in Africa is a family disease. Although AIDS enters the family through one person, it affects the physical, social, psychological, economic and spiritual well-being of all members of the family. The goal of this program was to offer quality terminal care—by family as well as community members—for patients dying from AIDS, and to meet the needs of the family by providing social, psychological and especially spiritual support throughout.

When patients were tested for the HIV infection in the hospital, they were told the results by a team consisting of a nurse and a chaplain. The nurse who started the program is an American missionary nurse attached to Chidamoyo Christian Hospital. The chaplain was a Bible college graduate from Zimbabwe Christian College in Harare, who was hired by the hospital specifically to be a chaplain to AIDS patients. The hospital was committed to integrating medical and spiritual care from the initial contact with the AIDS patients and their families. Family members, as well as the patient, were included in post-counseling sessions. Those patients in terminal stages were offered home care by the same team.

The home care team believed strongly that family members can give good quality care to a patient with AIDS as long as support continued from the hospital and community. The hospital responsibility for a patient with AIDS did not end with telling the patient he had AIDS or upon a patient's discharge from the hospital. Patients needed to be followed closely to try and limit the spread of the disease. The home care program would link the hospital to the community.

From the beginning the staff realized that there were too many patients in the program for the home care team to visit more than once a month. The team felt that this was not frequent enough. Many of the families were in shock adjusting to the news that a family member was dying from AIDS. Some of these patients had been major breadwinners working away from the home and had returned to their rural homes ill and dying. This was a traumatic time for the families and much support was needed.

The team also had other responsibilities at the hospital and were only able to initially invest one afternoon a week to visiting home care patients. The patients lived at times far distances from the hospital, making it impossible to visit more than three or four a week. The home care team felt it was impossible to offer the psychological and spiritual support needed during this period immediately after diagnosis, with so many people to see and so little time to do it.

The team quickly decided that the best people to involve in caring for the AIDS patients and their families were local Christians. Christians in the community are a caring group with an organized structure for reaching out to their community through churches.

There are 35 Churches of Christ congregations within a 60-mile radius of Chidamoyo Christian Hospital. The hospital staff decided in 1992 to train two women, two men and two youth from each of these congregations as a community team in their area, reaching out to AIDS patients with community and spiritual support. These teams would work with and supplement the home care team based at the hospital.

One-day workshops were held involving the team from each congregation. AIDS education—how the disease is spread, diagnosed and treated—was taught. Videos on AIDS and role playing of actual situations that may arise during home visits were presented. The home visits by the church members were to act only as psychological and spiritual support for the patient and the patient's family. The hospital team would provide the medical support that was needed. The church was to incorporate this ministry into their other outreach activities, as well as refer people that the hospital may not know about because they had come home ill from other areas.

The churches would also examine and look for solutions to issues that had arisen or would arise concerning the AIDS crisis, such as care of orphans, support of elderly grandparents raising young orphans, lack of food and help in caring for the patient at home. Churches were encouraged to come up with viable projects that would help to meet these needs.

The support for holding these workshops was provided by government funding as part of AIDS prevention and training in our area. The costs involved transportion and food for participants. The hospital cooked the food and provided overnight accommodation.

As patients were counseled with their families and were prepared for discharge, they were offered the services of the home care team. They were also offered the services of a group from the local church in their area to visit them. If they agreed, hospital staff notified the church leader in that area, and if possible arranged to pick church people up to go on the first home care visit with the team.

At the first visit the home care team would explain that the church team would be coming every week to visit. If there was any change in the patient's medical status, the family could let the church team know so that they could notify the home care team, or the family could send word to the hospital. The home care team explained the roles of the hospital and church teams.

The most important part of each visit is sharing and allowing patients and their families to talk about themselves, the disease and how they are coping. Time is spent reading from the Bible and praying with the patient and family. Spiritual support throughout the illness is important and comforting to the patient and his family.

One of the major results of this program has been the strengthening of the local churches in the Chidamoyo area. The patients and families are coming to know the Lord because of this acute crisis in their life. Many have the opportunity to hear the gospel presented to them for the first time as part of their counseling session when they are told they are infected with AIDS. Many have told us that they gave thought to what we said later and that it was comforting to them that we had prayed for them during the session.

Church members see people in crisis and present the gospel to them. Through their compassion and acts of mercy, AIDS patients are being accepted into the community without stigma, and the

psychological and spiritual support they receive helps many to
have a peaceful end to their lives.

Opportunities arise on many home visits to do health education
on prevention and behavior changes necessary for those who may
not be infected. Children, neighbors and family members are all
included in the visits and discussions. Preventing the spread of the
disease is an important part of education and sharing with community members. At times we have talked to groups of 50 or more
people. By seeing the reality of the disease in someone personally
known to them, the disease becomes more personal to the members
of a community.

Results of the program

Behavior change in sexual matters is hard to evaluate, but
change is slowly taking place. The home care team encourages
open discussion about AIDS and talks frankly with everyone present concerning what is wrong with the patient. Seeing the reality
of the disease in their own family has caused many to reevaluate
their lives and behavior, and it brings many to a point in their lives
where they are open to the gospel.

Visits are not limited to church members or to Christians. God's
love, compassion and comfort are for all. AIDS is not a condemnation from God. The church has a biblical mandate to console (2
Corinthians 1:3-5), to reconcile (2 Corinthians 5:19), to love (1
Corinthians 13:1-8) and to minister (Matthew 25:35-36, 40). The
home care team works with the local churches to help them to minister to these people with unconditional love. AIDS is in the church
in Africa, and many of the church members are already infected
and need the hope that Jesus Christ has to offer.

Cultural changes have started because of home care. The home
care team can talk about issues like *nhaka* (a brother inheriting his
brother's widow). This is a dangerous practice if the brother has
died of AIDS, as more family members may be infected. Open discussions with the family and emphasis on providing for the widow
and her children, without sexual union, take place. Handling of the
body during illness and in death has also been discussed to mini-

mize possible contamination of care givers. Many changes in burial practices, such as internal cleansing and washing of the body, are changing because of education.

Talking about care of children and informing women of their legal rights upon the death of their spouse are also important services of the home care team. Many times the husband's family takes everything away from the widow, including her children, and blame her for the death of her husband. Traditional culture believes there is someone who has caused this illness, and many times the wife is the one blamed by the husband's family.

In the past, talking about death meant that you wished the person to die. Now the team can have the patient and family talk about the eventuality of death and make plans for its occurrence. Much time is spent talking about not placing blame on who caused the illness, but on dealing with the illness and practicing forgiveness.

Process of people coming to know Christ

Through the presentation of the gospel in daily devotions and one-to-one sharing between patients and the hospital's chaplains and staff, many come to know the Lord. All three chaplains at the hospital have been trained in AIDS counseling and participate during counseling sessions with the patients. When patients are told of their HIV infection they are also presented the gospel as part of the counseling session. They are given material to study and read and are encouraged to continue talks with the chaplains.

Baptisms are held at the hospital chapel as people commit their lives to the Lord. Other patients at the hospital and local church members attend to offer support and encouragement.

The local congregation near the hospital has a women's group that comes to visit the patients in the hospital once a week. They are informed if any patient is from the local area so that they can call on him or her in the hospital. They sing, read from the Bible and pray with the patient and any family members that may be present.

The local church continues the process when the patient is discharged. During their visit they sing, read from the Bible and pray.

They talk about their church and invite family members to attend. The local members become involved in giving financial support as needed to families and orphans. They also take charge of many of the funeral services.

One new church has been started because of a husband and wife who came to know the Lord while they were being treated at Chidamoyo Christian Hospital three years ago. Ephraim and Juliet were both in their early thirties. Ephraim had been employed as a fisherman in Kariba for several years. When he lost his job he returned home and spent much time in a state of depression, going to the beer hall with his friends. He became sick and came to the hospital for treatment. It was found that both he and his wife had pulmonary tuberculosis and AIDS. They had three small children at home.

During their counseling session, when they were told they had AIDS and were presented with the gospel, Ephraim and Juliet accepted Christ and were baptized. Upon their discharge, they returned to their home in an area about 50 kilometers from Chidamoyo, where there was no church. We encouraged them to find a local church.

They returned for their checkup at the hospital one month later and said they had a group of 15 meeting at their village every Sunday for church. They wanted teaching materials, songbooks and Bibles. They were very excited by the change in their lives.

The home care team quickly made an evaluation trip to their area and arranged for a church leader from a nearby church to come every Saturday to spend the day teaching and calling on people in the area. He would then spend the night at the village and hold services the next day. Ephraim and Juliet promised to pay his bus fare back and forth and to provide him with food and a place to sleep.

Physically Juliet and Ephraim improved and were healed of their tuberculosis. They felt well and were able to function normally. Spiritually a great change took place in their lives, which was apparent to their families and to their community. They were able to talk openly about the changes in their lives. They visited at the hospital for their tuberculosis medication and each time were very excited in sharing about the progress of their new church.

One year later the home care team was invited to a special "celebration of life" service. The couple gave testimony to those who attended about the changes in their lives and how God had allowed them to live one year more than they thought possible. They felt they were going to die before they left the hospital. Ephraim's former drinking friends also testified that they had noticed the change in him and had asked him what was different. Many came to know the Lord because of Ephraim and Juliet.

Today there are more than 100 people regularly attending worship services at the home of Juliet and Ephraim, who are doing well. They have dedicated whatever time they have left to the Lord.

The churches in the Chidamoyo area have been strengthened because of the outreach into the community through the AIDS work being done by local churches. Many new members have been added and there have been more than 40 baptisms of AIDS patients in the past four years. A portable baptistry made of canvas has been bought to baptize patients at their own homes. Two of the established churches are being led by people with AIDS who were counseled through the hospital program and who felt the urgency and vibrancy of getting the message out to other people. They are young men who had not been attending church before they were diagnosed and counseled. They have changed their lives to live for the Lord no matter how much time they have left.

The churches feel they are coworkers with the hospital and can reach far more people in their community with the gospel and with support for families and patients living with AIDS. The churches are becoming stronger because of the care and concern shown by their members. The churches are in constant contact with the hospital concerning the condition of the patients, and if deaths occur they invite the hospital staff to come and share at the funeral. Funerals are large community gatherings, and the church's presence and message are felt during these times.

Evaluation of the case

The biggest improvement would be to make this a full-time program. There are approximately 40 patients in the program at all times and it could be expanded to serve even more patients and families, but the staff involved must also continue their full-time work at the hospital.

Since 1990 we have had a cumulative total of 2,358 new cases of HIV/AIDS. The home care team has been able to make a total of 408 home visits since April 1991, an average of 3.75 visits per family. This leaves many families who need to be in the program but who cannot be included because of a lack of personnel and time. The current home care team makes visits two afternoons a week.

There were no external obstacles to the program. The government and local churches were very supportive of the hospital's involvement in such a program. The program has received recognition by Zimbabwe's Ministry of Health for leadership and compassionate care offered to AIDS patients.

The most important part of integrating the spiritual ministry into our program was to make that a priority and to keep referring to the goals of the program on an ongoing basis. Many visitors to the program have seen the need for the spiritual care of AIDS patients. Through showing this need to many government and nongovernmental groups, many have adapted Bible reading and praying into their own home care programs, having seen the need expressed by patients and the comfort it offers.

Spiritual care as a component of AIDS home care has also been included in the national program for home care for AIDS patients through input from our program at national planning workshops. Most Zimbabweans are very spiritual people and seek spiritual care and comfort when they are ill. Even President Mugabe has called on the church to be in the forefront of the AIDS crisis.

Two government home care programs have asked for consultation concerning Bible verses to read to patients who are ill and Christian songs that would be good to sing. One private home care program bought a Bible to be used in their home care kits by their volunteers because they saw the importance of spiritual care and the comfort it brought to the patients and their families while visiting and seeing our program in action.

The program is run by Kathy McCarty, a nurse, and Major Mareki, a chaplain. We also integrate all of the nurses in the hospital into helping with the home visits and have added two more chaplains, a man and a woman, to meet the needs of our many AIDS patients.

Finances

The home care program has been totally financed by governmental funding for AIDS work. The program operated on $18,000 (Zimbabwean dollars) in 1991 and now has a budget of $30,000 a year. Most of the finances go toward transportation costs for the program and training programs for church leaders.

The government has not been constrictive about financing the program. Government financing has not in any way limited the preaching of the gospel. The government has been very supportive in financing the training of church leaders as community home care workers. The hospital convinced the government of the idea that church people had more of a commitment to people in their community than other people in the community. Most people are not as concerned and do not have time for others. The Christians in the area, however, have a desire to reach out to people because of their love and concern for people. The government has seen that the effective programs operating in the country are church-related home care programs.

During the home care visits, the hospital also gives food provided by the government from supplementary feeding programs. This is very important in a time of drought when families do not have enough food and sick patients need proper nutrition to survive.

The purpose of our program remains to lead people to a personal knowledge of Jesus Christ. Whether people have AIDS or not, we want to prevent people from dying without knowing the Lord. We feel privileged to have this opportunity in working with AIDS patients in Zimbabwe.

Appendix 1
Vision for Home Care Program
Chidamoyo Christian Hospital
Adopted April 1991

BELIEVING IN JESUS AS LORD, we affirm the message that God offers forgiveness to all through his Son, Jesus Christ. God wishes no one to perish but all to be saved. This is our goal throughout this program, as stated in Romans 8:1: "Therefore, there is now no condemnation for those who are in Christ Jesus . . . " We desire to undertake this program with the express purpose of bringing those patients with AIDS and their families to a personal knowledge of Jesus Christ.

We undertake this vision as follows:

1. Patients will be referred to the program by the medical staff working at Chidamoyo Christian Hospital and/or community or church members. First priority will be given to those patients in the terminal stage of AIDS.
2. Patients will be introduced to the Home Care staff while they are inpatients so that a personal relationship can be formed between Home Care staff and the patient and family.
3. Counseling sessions will also emphasize the hope that Jesus Christ is in our lives. Forgiveness is an essential part of this counseling and the gospel will be presented at each session with the patient and family.
4. Home visits will include medical care, psychological support for the patient and family dealing with AIDS, and spiritual support through prayer and Bible reading and presentation of the gospel to unbelievers, and encouragement of believers.
5. Supplementary food to help the patient nutritionally will be offered as available to those who are in need.
6. Liaison with the local church in the area will be arranged for those patients that do not have a local church. The local church will maintain weekly visits with the patient and family as part of their calling and outreach into the community.
7. We believe strongly in meeting the physical, psychological and spiritual needs of people with AIDS and their families within their communities and home. Community support for these patients will be encouraged at all times by education, prevention and openly talking about the disease.
8. We believe strongly that sexual behavior change is desirable and obtainable to stop the disease of AIDS. God has called us to sexual purity outside and inside marriage and it is important to present God's plan, without condemnation, to bring about change and hope to believers and nonbelievers alike.
9. The Home Care team will work closely together with the hospital staff for encouragement and help in meeting the needs of the patients and their fami-

lies in the hospital and at home after discharge. The Home Care team will also offer encouragement to the staff on their care and handling of the patients while in the hospital. The responsibility for providing compassionate, nonjudgmental care is upon all staff at Chidamoyo Christian Hospital and the Home Care Team.

10. The goal of our program at all times is to fulfill the biblical mandate:

   i. *To console*: "Blessed be the God and Father of our Lord Jesus Christ, the Father of mercies and God of all comfort, who comforts us in all our tribulation, that we may be able to comfort those who are in any trouble, with the comfort with which we ourselves are comforted by God. For as the sufferings of Christ abound in us, so our consolation also abounds through Christ" (2 Corinthians 1:3-5).

   ii. *To reconcile*: ". . . that is, that God was in Christ reconciling the world to Himself, not imputing their trespasses to them, and has committed to us the word of reconciliation"(2 Corinthians 5:19).

   iii. *To love*: "And though I bestow all my goods to feed the poor, and though I give my body to be burned, but have not love, it profits me nothing. Love suffers long and is kind; love does not envy; love does not parade itself, is not puffed up; does not behave rudely, does not seek its own, is not provoked, thinks no evil; does not rejoice in iniquity, but rejoices in the truth; bears all things, believes in all things, hopes all things, endures all things. Love never fails . . ." (1 Corinthians 13:3-8).

   iv. *To minister:* "For I was hungry and you gave Me food; I was thirsty and you gave Me drink; I was a stranger and you took Me in; I was naked and you clothed Me; I was sick and you visited Me; I was in prison and you came to Me. . . . And the King will answer and say to them 'Assuredly, I say to you, inasmuch as you did it to one of the least of these My brethren, you did it to Me'" (Matthew 25:35-36, 40).

5

Holistic lending by Zambuko Trust, Zimbabwe

Evans Maphenduka and Larry Reed

October 1992: The Mufakose Glad Tidings Church meets in a rented hall too small to accommodate its growing membership. While the adults worship inside the cramped room, the children learn their Sunday school lessons in the shade of a msasa tree. Despite the stifling heat of the packed room, the congregation grows each week. The energetic preaching of the pastor and elders in quarterly week-long crusades continually adds new converts to the church.

The crowds attending have led to an eviction notice by the landlord. The church has begun a drive to raise money for a new building, but to date has raised less than one-tenth of the estimated construction cost of US$50,000. The problem: only 62 of the 200 adults in the church have jobs. Most of these adults earn the minimum wage of US$50 per month, and many had been giving US$10 per month to build a new church. With construction costs escalating each month, there is no way that the church of 400 will raise enough funds to construct a new building unless more people in the congregation find jobs.

The pastor and the elders begin to address the problem of unemployment in the church. They preach sermons on the responsibility of Christians to provide for themselves and others. They raise a small fund to help church members acquire the tools they will need to start businesses. And they begin working closely with Zambuko Trust, a Christian organization that provides micro-enterprise (a business with five or fewer employess and less than US$5,000 in assets) loans and business training.

The reason for Zambuko Trust

Zambuko Trust was formed in late 1990 as a response by Christian business people and church leaders to the growing problem of unemployment in Zimbabwe. Zambuko has been supported in its development by Opportunity International in the U.S. and Opportunity Foundation in Australia.

The board of Zambuko see as their vision "a nation under God where all people have the dignity of providing for themselves, their families, their churches and their communities." They chose the name Zambuko, which means "bridge" in the Shona language, because the mission of the organization is ". . . to be a bridge between the underprivileged and opportunities for enterprise and income generation in our society."

Unemployment has become a widespread and growing problem in Zimbabwe. Currently Zimbabwe has almost two million unemployed persons (40 percent of the adult population). Partly in response to this problem, the government has introduced an Economic Structural Adjustment Programme (ESAP). In the short term, however, ESAP has seen increased unemployment as state-owned corporations and private companies shed employees in an attempt to compete in the world market.

In addition, Zimbabwe has just gone through several years of severe drought. Drought pushed people off their farmlands to seek employment in urban areas. Many have found conditions in the cities even worse than the situations they left. They have been unable to find jobs, yet face escalating prices in basic commodities brought on by ESAP and the drought.

The large number of unemployed people in the cities is having very distressing consequences. Robbery and violent crime have increased dramatically in the past three years. The cities also house a growing number of "street kids." These children, some as young as 6 years of age, spend their days in the city hustling for money. They mind cars, beg for food and sometimes engage in petty thievery to get enough money for a meal. Many have become addicted to glue sniffing, seeking relief from their hunger pains with a temporary high.

The future employment situation does not look bright. Even in good times the Zimbabwe economy has had trouble keeping pace with its growing population. Each year the Zimbabwe school system produces 300,000 school leavers (graduates and dropouts), while the formal economy in its pre-drought growth period was only expanding enough to create 30,000 new jobs a year.

The long term consequences of growing unemployment can be devastating to the country's plans for development. Unemployed people cannot purchase goods and services from others. Unemployed parents cannot supply adequate housing, food, health care or schooling for their children. Children who grow up with unemployed parents find it hard to overcome the disadvantages of their upbringing and have difficulty finding employment when they become adults. The government tries to address these problems through social welfare programs, but does not have enough funds to reach more than a small percentage of the affected population.

Unemployment can also wreak havoc on church ministries. When church members do not have jobs, they cannot contribute funds for church activities. Churches with large numbers of unemployed members have difficulty sustaining their own operations, let alone expanding their ministries. Pastors often need to take on one or two other jobs to earn enough money to provide for their families, limiting the time they have for evangelism or equipping the saints for ministry.

This was the dilemma faced by Glad Tidings Mufakose. The church had a vision for reaching the poor and unemployed in the densely populated, low income community in which they were located. They also had a vision for reaching beyond Mufakose into even poorer communities in rural areas. But as long as the members had no jobs, the church could not even find an adequate shelter for their meetings, let alone carry out an expanded ministry.

The one bright spot in Zimbabwe's employment picture has been the resilience and growth of small and micro-enterprises in the informal sector. According to a nationwide study conducted by the GEMINI program of USAID, there are over 845,000 small and micro-enterprises in Zimbabwe employing over 1.3 million people. This means that the small and micro-enterprise sector employs up to 60 percent of Zimbabwe's working population.[1]

These small and micro-enterprises have demonstrated their ability to create new jobs at a very low cost. On average, it takes $500 of investment to create one new job in the informal sector, as opposed to the $25,000 of investment it takes to create a new job in the formal sector.

The growth of this sector, however, has been constrained by an almost total lack of credit. The GEMINI study found that only 1 percent of the 845,000 small enterprises have ever received credit of any type from a financial institution. Small enterprise owners gave lack of access to credit, especially working capital, as one of the primary problems they face. Formal financial institutions and even the government-owned Small Enterprise Development Corporation do not make loans to small, unregistered micro businesses operating in the informal sector.

The church members in Mufakose understood this problem all too well. Ready and willing to work, they found their lack of five "O Level" passes (roughly equivalent to a high school diploma in the U.S.) made it impossible for them to get employment in established businesses. They had the skills to work on their own, but could not get the credit they needed from banks to buy the raw materials or equipment required to start or expand their own businesses.

The ministry of Zambuko Trust

Zambuko Trust provides loans and business training for those who cannot obtain credit from the banks. Zambuko's lending methodology supports the growth of micro-enterprise into small businesses through a system of graduated loans and targeted training. First loans to clients are generally for very small amounts over a short period of time. Zambuko bases these loans on a good business concept, work experience and a good character reference, but requires no collateral. By lending primarily to micro-enterprises that have been operating for six months or more, Zambuko avoids the large number of businesses that fail in their first few months. By making very small (under US$300) and short-term (4-6 months) first-time loans Zambuko meets the needs of very small enterprises for working capital, does not overextend their borrowing capacity and discourages borrowers who could qualify for loans from the banks.

Zambuko employs the "faithful with little" principle in making repeat loans to clients. Borrowers who repay their loans on time qualify for larger loans. Those who do not pay back on time have their loan amounts reduced or their credit privileges rescinded. Over time borrowers develop a credit history with Zambuko that reduces the risk of lending them much larger amounts of money. Thus, for those businesses that have the capacity to grow and a good repayment record, Zambuko can support their growth with ever-increasing loans until they qualify for credit from the formal financial sector.

Undergirding the credit program is Zambuko's training program. The first part of this training is a required pre-loan course that explains Zambuko's lending procedures and the responsibilities of borrowers. Zambuko also offers optional courses to borrowers in subjects such as marketing, personnel management, inventory control and basic accounting procedures. These training modules are designed to address common problems encountered by micro-enterprises as they grow into larger and more formal structures. Taught by Christian trainers, these courses use biblical examples and principles to address business themes.

Zambuko's methodology depends on the motivation, enterprise and hard work of its clients. It does not initiate any projects. Prospective clients come to Zambuko after they have already started their own small enterprises, and use the services Zambuko provides to expand their businesses and create new employment.

71

The results

Table 5.1 below shows the results of Zambuko's program to date in economic terms. What the table does not show is the true impact of Zambuko's program—the way the income generated from these small enterprises has led to improved quality of life for business owners, their families and their employees. It also does not show the impact on the church as church members provide tithes and offerings made possible by new employment.

One example may help to illustrate the wider impact of Zambuko's ministry. Terezia Mbasera took out one of the first loans provided by Zambuko. At that time she struggled to survive by selling eggs from the back of her rented house. She has now received five loans, for a combined total of less than US$5,000. With these loans she has expanded the tuck shop at the back of her house, opened a new corner store along a major walking path (she calls it her supermarket), set up a firewood stall, a beauty salon and a business manufacturing cool pops (which she sells in her supermarket). She has employed nine people in her various businesses and her daily sales have increased from Z$200 per day to over Z$2,000 per day.

The impact of *Ambuya* (Grandmother) Mbasera's businesses, however, goes far beyond these simple numbers. She also provides

	1992	1993	1994	1995	Total
Loans Made	269	449	2,194	3,600	6,512
Amt. Loaned (Z$)	$468,080	$812,745	$2,769,900	$4,772,207	$8,822,932
Loans to Women	175	226	1,295	2,125	3,821
Jobs Created	110	353	1,463	2,521	4,447
Jobs Sustained	362	836	1,816	3,129	6,143
Repayment Rate	99%	99%	97%	97%	97%

Table 5.1. Economic results of the Zambuko Trust Program

accommodation for all of her employees and three people from her church, housing them in premises she built with profits from her businesses. All of Ambuya Mbasera's employees have come to know Christ as a result of her witness. She has also challenged the elders of her church to provide better compensation to the pastor and increased her giving to help pay for it. Then she challenged all of the other members of the church to follow her example and give more than a 10 percent tithe each week.

Ambuya Mbasera's work in her church has had an impact on other congregations. She belongs to a Glad Tidings church. When she challenged her elders on compensation for her pastor, the denomination had to reconsider their compensation for all of the pastors in the denomination. The church in Mufakose used her as an example to challenge its members to work hard in business and increase their giving to the church.

Zambuko and Christian witness

Zambuko's work supports the growth of the church in three ways. First, Zambuko's staff find they often must address both spiritual and economic needs as they deal with their clients. An example: Lena Chitema meets with a client and explains the work of Zambuko Trust. She asks the client for the name of a pastor or community leader to supply a character reference. In return, the client asks Lena about where she goes to church and what she believes. Soon the two are bowed in prayer, as the client asks Christ into her life.

Second, Zambuko provides an expression of God's love in the marketplace. It relates the values of the Scriptures to the rough-and-tumble of buying and selling and making a profit. In doing this it helps those who attend church to realize that Christianity is not a Sunday only religion, but should affect the way believers live each day of their lives. Ambuya Mbasera demonstrates how this is done. She learns from Zambuko's training how biblical values relate to her commercial enterprises. Her expanding businesses give her the opportunity to witness to employees, clients and vendors.

73

Third, Zambuko helps build the economic base of the church. It teaches its Christian clients that they have a responsibility to give a portion of their profits to the church (it also encourages non-Christian clients to give to community activities). This results in increased income to the church, which allows it to carry out expanded ministry. This increased income also allows local churches to develop their own plans for church growth, rather than being dependent on the funds and plans of outside donors. This is the sort of impact the church in Mufakose desired when it began referring its members to Zambuko.

Our interviews with loan officers suggest that the witness of the Zambuko staff leads to 10-20 people each month making a commitment to Christ. While this part of Zambuko's Christian witness is the most easily measured, it probably has less of a long-term impact than the other two areas. The larger impact of Zambuko comes through the witness of Zambuko's Christian clients and the expanded ministry of the church made possible by the increased giving from Zambuko's clients. The indirectness of this impact makes it less measurable, but the examples of the Mufakose church and Ambuya Mbasera show how profound it can be.

Zambuko could improve the impact of its witness in the other two areas by making sure its Christian clients and their pastors have the tools and knowledge to use Zambuko effectively. For example, Zambuko could develop special training materials for Christian borrowers that would show them how to minister to their employees and clients. Zambuko could also develop training programs for pastors. It could use people like the pastor of the Mufakose church to explain how the economic development of church members could help fuel the growth of the church and its ministries.

Key issues

Two issues affect the Christian witness of Zambuko's microenterprise development program. The first has to do with the mixing of the provision of an economic benefit with a gospel message. The second has to do with Zambuko's sources of funding and the restrictions they place on Christian witness.

The loans provided by Zambuko can make the difference between whether a mother can earn enough to provide regular meals for her children or not. They may decide whether a father can send his children to school. For this reason people will often do whatever they think it takes to receive a loan. This makes Zambuko very wary of creating the impression that people will have a better chance of getting a loan if they become Christians in the process. It has no more desire to create "credit Christians" than refugee ministries have to create "rice Christians."

The staff of Zambuko take pains to explain to Zambuko's clients that loan decisions are based on the viability of the business and the character of the applicant, and not on expressions of faith or church membership. It does not include evangelistic messages in its training programs. When such conversions do take place they occur because the example of the organization and its staff prompts questions by the clients.

Zambuko receives over three-quarters of its funding from government donors that prohibit the use of their funds for religious purposes. In many cases these donors try to establish a secular-spiritual divide that Africans find baffling. Most Zambuko clients will talk about spiritual issues as readily as they talk about the weather, and find biblical examples in training programs helpful in explaining business concepts. Yet Zambuko donors get squeamish when they think about the Bible being used in a training class or the loans having an impact on the growth of the church. So far Zambuko has avoided problems with these donors by maintaining its strict policy that loans be made available to all people, regardless of their religious beliefs.

For the clients in Mufakose, the source of Zambuko's funds makes little difference. While government donors may place restrictions on how Zambuko uses their funding, they can place no controls on how Zambuko's clients use their expanded profits. These clients had the freedom to give all they wanted to the construction of a new church in their community.

But is it Christian?

While Zambuko sometimes has trouble with government donors over its Christian nature, it more often has trouble convincing church leaders, especially those from the West, that it really is Christian. Zambuko deals in the most material of all commodities—money. It hires loan officers, not evangelists. It provides loans, not grants, and expects its clients to pay back these loans with interest. For many in the church it is hard to relate Zambuko's work with the traditional image of Christian ministry.

But looked at in another way, Zambuko not only demonstrates true Christian concern for the whole person, it also makes it possible for holistic ministry to take place in its most traditional form. At the very beginning of the Christian church the disciples appointed leaders who would take care of the needs of the people in their midst (Acts 6). One of the distinguishing characteristics of the first century church was that it not only cared for the needs of its members, but also the needs of nonbelievers in the community. People in the church shared their resources to make sure that poor people in the church and in the surrounding community received the help they needed. This witness of the church helped to fuel its growth.

In the modern era we have moved away from this type of holistic ministry. Instead, we have large-scale projects led by people who come from far continents. The assistance is provided in the name of Christ and from the church universal, but it often bypasses the local church on its way to the people in need. This can lead to humanitarian assistance provided in a very competent and professional manner that provides little impact on the growth of the local church. It leaves no Christian community on the ground to continue the ministry after the international organization has left.

Some Christian agencies seek greater church involvement by channeling their funds and development work through local churches. But this can create a whole new set of problems. The church becomes accountable to outsiders, who may not know the local culture or economy, for the ministry it carries out in its community. The scale of the funding creates temptations and tensions that can destroy the ministry the donor sought to expand.

Zambuko's method is different. It seeks to build the capacity of the local church to carry out holistic ministry, to enable the church to reach out with the love of Christ to all who suffer in its midst. When the money the church uses for ministry comes from the work of its members' hands, the church knows the value of those funds. Members will hold pastors and elders accountable for the wise use of the money they have contributed.

Holistic ministry in Mufakose and other parts of the world requires money, just as it did for the Good Samaritan. When the unemployed fill the church pews, the church does not have the money to carry out this ministry. Zambuko's loans and business training enable church members to work, and so fulfill the instructions given by Paul to the church in Thessalonica:

> *Now about brotherly love we do not need to write to you, for you yourselves have been taught by God to love each other. And in fact, you do love all the brothers throughout Macedonia. Yet we urge you, brothers, to do so more and more. Make it your ambition to lead a quiet life, to mind your own business and to work with your hands, just as we told you, so that your daily life may win the respect of outsiders and so that you will not be dependent on anybody (1 Thessalonians 4:9-12).*

Epilogue

October 1995: Construction workers begin roofing the spacious new church building of the Mufakose Glad Tidings congregation. The two-story church, with its facing of red brick, stands like a beacon over the crowded, low income suburb of Mufakose. Its ground floor seats 800 and its balcony another 200. One wing houses a training school used to develop pastors for new churches being planted in outlying rural areas. For the past three years the Mufakose Glad Tidings congregation, now grown from 400 to over 800, has met under a shade cloth on the building site, anxiously awaiting the completion of their new church.

Where did the church find the funds for its magnificent new building? Over half came from the contributions of its members, and the remainder came in the form of a loan from International

Cooperating Ministries in the U.S. The Mufakose church members will repay this loan to a church building fund to help construct the churches in rural areas.

How did the church members come up with the money to qualify for the loan and pay for the construction? From their own income. Where three years ago only 62 church members had employment, today every household head in the congregation (more than 300 in all) has an income-earning job.

And how did all the unemployed adults in the congregation find jobs? First, through the work of the pastors and elders of the church who preached on the importance of work and sought out employment opportunities for their members. Second, through the loans and business training provided by Zambuko Trust to members of the church, enabling them to expand their small businesses and employ other church members.

The funds the church used on the building came from special offerings designated for that purpose. The regular tithes and offerings allowed the church to carry out its normal ministries, including providing for the widows and orphans in its community. The church's regular evangelistic services and demonstrated concern for all people in the community have caused its dramatic growth. And the work of Zambuko Trust has played a key part in enabling the church to fund its own holistic ministry.

NOTES

1   Michael McPherson, *Micro and Small-Scale Enterprises in Zimbabwe: Results of a Country-Wide Survey* (Bethesda: GEMINI, DAI, 1991).

6

Rushinga cattle project in Zimbabwe

Denias B. Musona

Between 1982 and 1984, the Rushinga District, located in Zimbabwe on the border with Mozambique, was flooded by a tide of Mozambican refugees escaping their country's civil war. The total population in the Rushinga area increased by about 5,000 as 100-300 refugees per day entered the area. There were no camps or facilities to support these refugees as the government's camps opened later, in 1985.

The "growth point" (a population center designated by the government as a place where growth is occurring) of Burai became the first stopping point for many Mozambicans. Burai is located 6 kilometers from the Mozambican border and is the first location, after crossing the border, to boast of shops and a local hospital.

With no support structures in place to welcome the refugees, the existing social structure and resource base were taxed to the breaking point. For entertainment and relaxation, local Zimbabweans were accustomed to brewing beer and then gathering to share a drink and a story. This became impossible as desperate Mozambican refugees would often steal the beer. Theft in general increased as local animals and other goods became sustenance for Mozambicans who had not yet been offered legitimate ways of making a living. As the area was experiencing a drought, local Zimbabweans were already pressed to find food that would take the place of their normal diet of mealie meal and vegetables of either the wild leaf or the garden variety. The emergency local diet of wild grasses and fruit from the baobab tree also became the diet for the refugees, thereby depleting the supply for local villagers.

At that time, food became so scarce that even wild crickets, which subsist on crops that had long dried up, were not to be found. This scarcity in food supply led to another form of theft. Businessmen from neighboring communities, aware of the great need caused by the drought, would barter mealie meal in return for the villagers' cattle. The rate at which they traded was one bag of mealie meal for one cow, whereas the actual market rate would have been twice that amount.

In rural Zimbabwe, to be rich means to own cattle. For farmers unable to purchase tractors, cattle serve as the means of weeding and plowing fields. Cattle provide milk for nourishing families, especially children. When young boys are grown and ready to marry, cattle serve as the *lobola* or bride price. In cases of emergency, cattle may be sold to provide much needed finances. In essence, to have a cow is to have everything.

Cattle were at the heart of a suspicion against outsiders held by the local community in Rushinga. During the war for Zimbabwean independence in the 1970s, Rushinga was the location of a ZANU PF (Zimbabwean African National Unity Patriotic Front) camp. When local villagers were forced to feed the soldiers, many locals lost most of their cattle, garden produce and other belongings. Many of the cattle that were not fed directly to the ZANU PF soldiers were poisoned by government soldiers, in the name of vaccination, so as not to end up as food for ZANU PF soldiers. These incidents created within the community feelings of suspicion and distrust toward anyone who wanted to have any involvement at all with their cattle.

On top of the distress provoked by the war and the large numbers of refugees entering Rushinga, the drought was creating other urgent needs among the local population. Without water, many people were going two to three days without a meal, families were separating as men traveled to look for work to earn cash for mealie meal and many children did not have the physical strength to attend school. Instead, the older children would spend their days searching for wild foods while the younger ones remained at home.

The Macedonian call

As the staff of the United Baptist Church attempted to learn more about the needs in the Rushinga area, one of the community leaders we met was Mr. Karema. A Malawian by birth, he was serving as a teacher for the Bopoma Primary School. During a long talk over lunch, he told us about the situation in Rushinga. He invited us to visit, which we did in February 1984.

During our visit, we met many of the local community members and leaders from Burai and the surrounding villages, named after their chiefs, Chitange and Mukosa. While discussing the situation in the area, we came to realize that the need was too big for us.

After the meeting in Rushinga we returned to Harare to share the situation with our head office staff. They agreed that we needed to do something for the people of Rushinga.

To fund the work, Mr. Curtis, an Australian church planter who worked with us in Zimbabwe from 1981 through 1989, and I contacted the TEAR Fund of Australia. They agreed to support us financially and with gifts-in-kind. During 1984 they provided us with a grant aimed at starting a food distribution program, with used clothing and with money designated specifically for building a home for the pastor we sent to Burai.

The test year for TEAR funding was 1984. They have renewed their assistance to us each year since then, with the level of assistance varying according to our ability to find local forms of support. As TEAR Fund is a Christian organization, they did not place any restrictions regarding Christian witness on the use of the funds. They support the fact, however, that we assist all people, regardless of whether they are Christians or not.

Phase I: Food distribution

In May 1984 we started the feeding and the outreach program. The decision to start our work with a feeding program was based on the needs expressed by the community members themselves.

After meeting with community leaders in February 1984, we used the "PRA" (participatory rural appraisal) method to assess and prioritize the needs of the community. A group of about 20 key community leaders, including teachers, the *kraal* head and businessmen, met together to identify the needs of their community. As a local teacher, Mr. Karema played a helpful role in this process.

The needs were identified and prioritized, with food as the most urgent need, water second, cattle third and clothing fourth. As we determined that the needs were too overwhelming for us to meet at once, we decided to commit to a long-term process that would address needs over a period of time, in the order they were listed.

To staff the distribution program we found three young men, all school leavers from Harare, who committed themselves to moving to Burai and remaining there throughout the end of the first phase of food distribution in 1985. These men would distribute food from 7:00 A.M. to 5:00 P.M. or 6:00 P.M., until the refugees stopped arriving for the day. As committed Christians from the United Baptist Church, they would always give devotions before their distributions. Receiving food was never contingent on whether or not a person was or became a Christian; rather, the devotions served as a way to commit the day's work to the Lord. This act, however, intrigued many people, who came forward expressing a desire to know more about Christ.

The food distribution program was aimed at aiding both the locals and the Mozambican refugees. After initial attempts at assessing who in the community needed this assistance, we gave up and decided that this type of assessment was a waste of time because everyone needed support. At that time, rural areas in Zimbabwe were not yet benefitting from any form of government assistance, because the Zimbabwean government was still too new and did not begin assistance until 1985.

Initially, it was the Mozambicans who were the most eager to receive rations; the locals remained suspicious of our motives. By June, however, after discussions with local community leaders, both Mozambicans and locals were coming in full force. At this point, we were purchasing and distributing sixty tons of mealie meal a week from the National Foods Company.

In November, we received secondhand clothing sent by both local and Australian churches in response to our sharing the need with them. Along with the mealie meal and the clothing, we also distributed beans, salt and *kapenda* (small dried fish) sent to us by the Red Cross of Zimbabwe, with whom we had begun to partner. In addition to the regular distribution program, we began a program for children under age five and a supplementary feeding program for children in grades one through five. The under-five's received a daily ration of porridge and beans, and those in grades one through five daily received a plate of beans or cooked ground nuts and a cup of *maheu*, a drink made of sorghum. We also drilled a number of bore holes in response to the people's request for water.

Also in November, the fruits of the morning devotions began to flourish as those who had become Christians joined to write us a letter asking us to send them a full-time pastor who would lead and teach the Word of God to the community. As an initial response, we visited Burai along with an evangelistic team. We spent two weeks there, and many gave their lives to Christ.

Our commitment to work in the Rushinga area, however, had prepared us to commit to increasingly deeper levels of involvement in the community. During the time I spent in Burai, my heart was touched by what I saw. I felt that the Lord was calling me there so I applied and was accepted for the position of pastor. From 1981-84 I had served as a pastor in Harare, so the transition to Burai was not an easy one. I had seen the difficult life that the people in Burai lived; I had seen the way they awoke at 2:00 A.M. to collect water to avoid waiting five to six hours in line during the day.

It was a challenge to convey my sense of call to my wife, but she and our two children joined me. Her sense of calling grew as she came to know the women of the area. She discovered that with the drought, the women could no longer work the fields, and they often spent hours in gossip and beer making. She worked with them to form groups and taught them knitting and dressmaking. Because most of these women could not read or write, she creatively used tree branches of different sizes to measure pieces of cloth as she taught them to sew.

Phase II: From relief to rehabilitation

During late 1985, several things happened that moved us on to the next phase of our ministry. First, the government began opening refugee camps for the Mozambicans, so they no longer relied on our support for their survival, and our ministry began to focus on the needs of the local Zimbabweans. Second, the rains came, people were able to gather a good harvest and our distribution program was reduced to a supplementary feeding program. Third, members of the local community began approaching us with requests for loans to purchase cattle.

The need for cattle had initially been identified as the third most urgent need, so the fact that the people were now requesting assistance in purchasing cattle indicated to us that the time had come to address this need. We started small by focusing on the 38-member Marombe-Burai cooperative. One of the first cooperatives registered in Zimbabwe, it had been formed by members of the community to improve their farming systems. They approached us requesting loans for cattle, plows and fertilizer.

In response, we provided them with four bulls, six heifers, plows, seeds and fertilizers. With these, they produced six acres of cotton in their first market crop in 1986. Although they made a good profit with their crop, they were forced to abandon their fields in June 1987 as RENAMO (Mozambican National Resistance) soldiers entered Zimbabwe, threatening Zimbabweans they accused of assisting the government forces, FRELIMO (Mozambican Liberation Front.)

Once the people abandoned their fields, the government relocated the cooperative to a large farm in the Mount Darwin area, 150 kilometers from Burai. As most of the 38 cooperative members were among those who had accepted Christ during the food distributions, they formed a home worship group in their new location. In time, and in partnership with the United Baptist Church, they organized themselves into a church, with elected elders, deacons and official membership in the Baptist Association. As of June 1995, they were 60 members strong as other families from the Mount Darwin farming area have joined the worshiping community. They have requested a full-time pastor and are currently receiving regular visits from our pastor based in neighboring Bindura.

As a result of the successful crops produced by the Marombe-Burai Cooperative, many other families came to us with requests for loans for cattle. We were able to assist 17 of these families.

Phase III: Rehabilitation to development

During the war in Mozambique, the Zimbabwean government had resettled many Zimbabweans located in the border regions into protected villages. In 1994, after the war had ended and the government had determined it was safe, people were settled back into their home locations. As people settled, those who had not yet benefitted from our programs, but who had seen our work in other areas, began to request loans for cattle.

These were new areas, so we once again used the PRA to partner with these communities in assessing their needs. The most urgent need identified was the need for economic security. In response to this need, we came up with a new approach to lending cattle. The actual project is called the "Rushinga Cattle Project." The problem with our old method of lending cattle was that it did not allow for a rapid turnover of the cattle. By the time the cattle were paid for, their cost had risen and so the total number of cattle in the program was continually declining.

With the new approach, payment occurs when a family that has received cattle passes on a newborn heifer to the next family in the program. Payments for the heifers go to a community fund that will be used for projects within the community. The community has decided that the money in this fund should be kept in a bank, for security and to earn interest. To start the cycle in May 1995, we bought fifty heifers and two bulls. Already ten heifers have given birth to six female calves and four bulls, and the community is very excited about the approach.

In this project, the community has elected their own leaders to be the supervisors. Their role is to ensure the smooth running of the program, seeing that the cattle are well taken care of and choosing which families should receive cattle. Our role as United Baptist staff is to facilitate their work, assisting them in writing funding proposals to donors and encouraging project sustainability. We do this by continually linking the community and the donors. We are also encouraging them to make the major decisions in the program, such as how and where to bank their money. With the level of enthusiasm and community participation already evident in this project, I can say it is one of our best yet.

Results of the program

The Marombe-Burai cooperative now has 22 head of cattle. With these cattle to plow their fields, they are growing maize, tobacco and sunflower. The produce from these fields not only provides subsistence for the families, but also cash as the crops are marketed. The success the cooperative members are experiencing with their fields has led them to look for financing for more ambitious market projects. Their livelihoods have improved so that they are now strong church supporters. In addition to regular tithes, they have provided maize and even a cow to our annual national church meetings. In these offerings, the initial assistance we provided to them has come full circle, reaching the point where the daughter church is now providing support to the mother church.

In addition to these changes, there have also been changes in the lives of those 17 families that we assisted with cattle. The original heifer or bull provided has grown to three or more cattle for many of these families. There is a considerable difference in the lives of those who received loans versus those who did not. The families who received cattle are now considered rich. They have been able to pay school fees for their children, they have done early plowing to have early crops, they have been able to build sturdy homes and they have financial support in the case of an urgent need.

In terms of spiritual change, in the Rushinga area alone we now have seven churches with one full-time pastor, who was recruited to replace me when I left in 1990. Some of these churches meet under trees, some meet in classrooms. They are all congregations that began during the food distributions. Several of these are small groups, having eight or so regular attenders, while a few of these congregations have a membership of 120-150. These seven churches represent growth from the original group of 250 believers who were baptized at Burai. Out of this group of believers have come three full-time pastors, trained within the Baptist church.

Within the structure of the United Baptist Church, changes have also occurred as a result of the Rushinga programs. In 1989, we set up a development desk staffed by full-time workers trained in community development. In 1990, when I moved to Harare, I became the chairman of the Development and Holistic Ministry Committee. I also function as the development coordinator for the church nationwide. Our development staff work alongside the evangelistic teams, carrying out needs assessments while they do evangelism. It used to be that we did evangelism only, but we now feel that evangelism with no concern for physical needs is like ministering to a ghost that needs no food, shelter or clothing. So we challenge ourselves to balance spiritual needs with physical needs.

Currently, we have three full-time development staff members who focus efforts on various districts within Zimbabwe. One of these staff members is the Rushinga-based pastor. The second is a development officer from Chimanimani who is based in the head office along with our third officer, who is also from Zimbabwe.

Process of people coming to know Christ

When the United Baptist Church began investigating the possibility of establishing a church in Burai, we discovered that most of the other evangelical churches worked only up to the Rushinga district offices. That is, where the tar road ends, church planting also ended. Where the dirt roads began, the only established churches were the Catholic and Zionist churches. We decided that we could have a strategic presence as an evangelical church in this new location ministering both physically and spiritually to the poor.

Through the witness of the three young men staffing the food distribution combined with the witness of the evangelistic team, 500 people accepted Christ during 1984. Most people accepted the Lord as individuals. Occasionally families came forward together, but we found that in a number of those cases, either the husband had forced the wife along or the mother had forced the children. There was one case where a whole village accepted Christ together. I had spoken to the head man of the Chiero village, and he brought the whole village together to meet with us. After I had shared the gospel with them and asked who wanted to receive Christ, all forty village members stood up. We felt that some of them had accepted out of pressure, but time told who had made a genuine commitment as some fell away and others remained steady.

Our strategy in working with these new believers was to gather them into classes, teaching them Christian beliefs throughout a full year. At the end of the year, they each had the opportunity to share what they had learned. These classes were taught by the three distribution staff, myself and visiting teams from Harare. By year's end, there were 250 people who had remained committed Christians and who were ready to be baptized. Others had fallen away with the pressures of the drought and the need to leave Burai to search for work.

This was the first baptism we held in the Rushinga area and it was a moving time for all who attended. Most of those who were to be baptized brought charms and other traditional worship material that had been given to them by the n'angas (witch doctors) for protection. We burned all of these things to demonstrate a visible end to that way of life. As the charms and tokens went up in flames, the non-Christians present commented on the power of a God who could have these things burned in his name and not suffer any damage from the spirits as a result. Although our first baptism in Rushinga was the most spectacular in size, the baptisms have continued each year since then.

In 1986 Chief Chitange, who we had first met during our initial visit to Burai in 1984, gave his life to the Lord. As a chief he faces unique struggles, since part of his role is to consult the spirits on behalf of community members when they have a need. Local tradition is for those who have a need to offer the chief money and then gather at his home for a meal while awaiting word through him. Chief Chitange still struggles with his role in the community now that he is a Christian.

We have encountered traditional beliefs in a number of shapes and sizes during our work in Rushinga. Belief in possession by the spirits of ancestors is common. In one family, we found a 5-year-old girl who was believed to be possessed by the spirit of her grandmother. Family members referred to her and revered her as their *ambuya* or grandmother and would consult her for their problems.

In another family, a 14-year-old girl was possessed by a spirit that caused her to break out in a horrible rash every time she bathed with cold water. The spirit said it would kill her if it was cast out. We invited pastors from Harare to come and pray with us for this girl and during a prayer meeting that lasted a whole night, the Lord cast out the spirit. The girl is now fine and healthy.

As people have come to the Lord, they have been able to regain lost dignity and establish their proper places within family structures.

An occurrence that has expanded the church has been the dispersion of people from the Burai area. For example, some of the teachers who were involved in the first PRA needs assessment in Burai, and who later accepted Christ, have been transferred to new schools as the population has shifted. They are still spreading the gospel and we have kept in touch with them.

Another example is the people who have moved to the Bindura and Shava Mines areas in search of employment. Again, these were people who had accepted the Lord during the food distributions. They have formed home groups and at their request, we sent a full-time pastor there in 1989. We have also formed a dressmaking group in Bindura and have sent two women to train the people full-time in dressmaking.

We thank God for the relief program begun in 1984 and for the development efforts that have continued since then. These efforts have enabled us to know our people and to have a time of sharing together, both physically and spiritually. As we have considered the results of combining these two aspects of ministry, we have found that the church in Rushinga has grown faster than any of our churches throughout the country. The "Rushinga Approach"— that of assessing needs first and then doing evangelism—has now become our model in many of the locations where we work.

There have been three men in particular who have played a key role in church expansion. These three became Christians and emerged from the Rushinga Development Program as men who were committed to the church and interested in being trained as pastors. In response, we paid their school fees and supported them through three years at the Baptist College in Zimbabwe. Pastor Matimura is currently pastoring in Marondera, Pastor Mutegede in the Rushinga area and Pastor Chiware is the school chaplain at Biri-iri High School in Chimanimani.

As a result of seeing the effectiveness of pastors who are committed to community development, the United Baptist Church has decided to train pastors in development while they are still at college. Development is now a course at the Bible college, and during school breaks students are taken to projects to see how they work. We even have a group of students who, after visiting the projects, began a project of their own to raise oranges and bananas. The profits from this project have gone to pay for school fees and buy books.

Evaluation of the case

In terms of meeting the community's physical needs, the boreholes we dug are sufficient for meeting community needs, but they are not economical for meeting family needs. We are currently seeking funds to construct a community dam for animal usage and family and community gardens. Gardens are essential in the Rushinga area, where the nearest place to buy green vegetables is 150-200 kilometers away.

We also found that it was most successful to work hand in hand with local community members. In many of the places where we had missionary workers, community members would tell the missionaries what they thought they wanted to hear. We tried to encourage open communication with the communities and to teach them to acknowledge their own mistakes.

One of the first problems we faced was due to the political situation at the time. In 1984, presidential candidates were busy campaigning for election. Our food distribution program came under suspicion because people thought we were feeding them to win their votes. We had already begun to develop a relationship with the district administrator and the social welfare officer, so we met with them and shared the problems we were facing. In response, they came to Burai to address the community and assure them that we had nothing to do with politics. Along with their support, we had support from another community elder, whose comments to the community I still remember: "Are you people not dying? If you know which party you will vote for, take the mealie meal from whoever is giving it out and on voting day, go ahead and vote for the party you want to vote for." Thankfully, the community's suspicions were eased by these assurances.

Transport of mealie meal and cattle was also a problem. I remember once when the truck transporting the cattle arrived after dark. As they were being unloaded from the truck, four of the cattle ran off into the bush. It took us four days to find them again.

Finding skilled supervision for community programs as well as developing management capacity in our head office have also been areas needing improvement. Financial support from the TEAR Fund has allowed us to invite experienced trainers to work with our staff in leadership, community relations, bookkeeping, administration and communication.

Some traditional beliefs were obstacles to successful development. When we arrived in Rushinga, people were not using grinding mills, which gave off diesel fumes, or chemicals in their cotton fields. They felt that this would disturb their ancestors. To confront these beliefs, we showed the people how use of a grinding mill could save them time and effort, and how they could move beyond subsistence farming to cash crop marketing by using fertilizer in their cotton fields. These discoveries, combined with their Christian faith, served to change these beliefs.

In conclusion, we in the United Baptist Church have discovered that before our involvement in the Rushinga community, we were going, as commanded in Matthew 28:19-20, but we were not taking the full gospel with us. We now teach students in the Bible college and pastors in the communities where we are present that the good news includes development. We want to minister to the whole person and meet physical, spiritual, social and economic needs.

I thank God for the opportunity to work in Rushinga. I have seen blessings returned to us many times over. The lives of many people have changed in so many ways, both physical and spiritual. There is a big difference between the places where we have worked and those places where we have not. This serves as a constant motivation for us to continue our ministry.

7
Reaching the lost through community health in Ghana

John Oduro Boateng

The Luke Society works in Ejura Sekyeredumasi District, Ashanti Province, Ghana. The government formally established this district in 1986 by combining two of the most deprived districts in Ashanti.

When the Luke Society entered this rural district in 1989, we found that there were only two health centers for the entire region and no doctors. I am a Ghanaian, raised in Ghana. I became the first director of the Luke Society's work in Ghana and was assigned to Ejura as its first physician, serving a population of 100,000.

The roads in the district were extremely rough, making travel to the market and access to medical or other care difficult. The district had no electricity, which is still limited to date. Most of the water came from shallow wells, which dried up every season. The educational system was not well developed. Since the people of the area are primarily farmers, they need their children to work with them at home and so many children would not attend the schools available to them. Finally, out of the 100 communities within the region, only five had Christian churches.

As a result of these conditions, many diseases were endemic to the region, including malaria and water borne diseases like diarrhea and intestinal parasites. Infant mortality was very high at approximately 30 per 1,000 live births.

In terms of economic conditions, Ghana is a resource-rich country, which makes the poverty of this region a tragedy that could have been avoided. Ghana is the second largest producer of gold in the world and among its natural riches are bauxite, manganese, cocoa, corn and pineapple.

In 1957, Ghana became the first African colony to gain its independence. It has continued to maintain a leadership position among African countries. Ghana was one of the first countries on the continent to begin an economic structural program with the World Bank and the International Monetary Fund, and was viewed as a test case. With reforms and an increased availability of resources, Ghana has had one of the fastest growing economies on the continent. Since 1983, GDP (gross domestic product) in constant prices has increased an average of 5 percent per year.

Ghana's economic reform program, which focused on increasing exports, has led to widespread unemployment as protected businesses and state-owned companies laid off employees to become competitive. Economic reform has also caused 25-35 percent inflation, as the price of imports rose in response to the devaluation of the currency. In 1987, World Bank figures showed that 36 percent of Ghanaians fell below the poverty line.

Ghana, however, has one of the most vibrant informal sectors in all of Africa. This sector provides more employment than any other sector of the economy. Lack of credit, however, constrains the growth of this sector. For this reason, the government is initiating programs that support development of small businesses, cooperative marketing efforts and credit unions.

Traditional religious practices, which promote idolatry and demonic bondage, are one of the factors prohibiting prosperity and well-being within the country. Much of the income and energy that could be going to support economic development is going instead to the construction of fetish shrines, black stools with gold storage used in traditional worship and expensive religious festivals. In some instances, shrines are located in places that block construction of much needed access roads. In other instances, community chiefs and elders are antagonistic to health and evangelism programs due to fear of their interaction with traditional health practices.

The religious practices and spiritual beliefs of community members in this region also account for many illnesses. Their traditional religions include animism, ancestral worship and fetish worship—the belief that spirits inhabit streams, rocks or other inanimate objects. Witches, wizards and fetish priests and priestesses hold great power over the people, inspiring fear rather than confidence. Many claim to be "healers," prescribing "medicines" for some and casting curses over others. This creates an environment in which people are less likely to turn to modern medical care for support.

Description of the program

The vision for the work came as a result of the combination of my own dreams and goals and those of the Luke Society. The Luke Society works internationally, reaching out to those who do not know Christ through community health and evangelism. I had a growing vision to help the poor among my own people in Ghana through health care and evangelism. A friend put the two of us in touch and we found we shared similar visions. In 1989, the Luke Society agreed to help fund a holistic health care program in the Ejura Sekyeredumasi region.

That year, I moved to Kasei in Ashanti Province and opened a medical clinic in a five-room house with no electricity. Clinic staff consisted of myself, my wife and one helper. We provided basic medical services, began training community health workers to teach basic sanitation, hygiene and disease prevention in the villages and held open air evangelism meetings in the evenings.

That was six years ago. In June 1994, the Luke Society in Ghana celebrated its fifth anniversary. By the grace of God, the clinic that began as a house with no electricity has expanded to encompass a compound which covers 30 acres, and includes a newly constructed medical clinic, our home, a hostel for inpatients, a canteen and a bath house.

The Luke Society in Ghana has four components: health delivery, evangelistic outreach, income generation projects and collaborative links. The stories below help to illustrate these aspects of the work.

Health delivery: Clinic and health centers

It is six o'clock on Monday morning. The waiting area outside the Kasei Clinic is full of men, women and children who have traveled from villages all around Ashanti Province, some from as far as the Ivory Coast. My staff and I began the day with devotions at 5 A.M. and I am already into my second hernia surgery. I will do 12 of these operations before the day is over. This is a common injury in this region because of the hard work the people do. Because many are farmers, lifting heavy loads is a part of their daily routine.

The technique used in the operation uses local rather than general anesthesia, so patients are conscious during the course of the operation. Clinic staff play Christian music, Bible teaching tapes and witness to the patients, even during the actual operation. Because of this, many people become Christians while they are being operated on.

In the next room, another medical officer, Peter Adom Asare, is examining patients who have a variety of complaints, from skin rash to fever. Many of them are suffering from malaria, a serious problem in the Ashanti Region. Nurse assistants Deborah Attwomaa and Regina Tizawe Mensal are dispensing medicine, much of which was donated and so can be provided to people at a very low cost.

The Kasei Clinic has a reputation for quality care. Because staff are careful with equipment and techniques, there is an almost 0 percent infection rate on hernia surgeries and very few patients have recurring hernias. This reputation extends into neighboring countries, drawing wealthy businessmen from the Ivory Coast and Burkina Faso. Because the clinic charges a fee based on ability to pay, the wealthy help to finance the cost of caring for those who cannot pay at all.

It is the poor that make up a large percentage of the practice. As you walk through the compound, you see people sitting under trees and recovering from illness or surgery. The people who need medical care the most, however, are often those who cannot come to the clinics. For that reason, the Luke Society has founded community health centers in 22 remote communities. Each center has one or more trained community health workers and a dispensary. Five of the centers, in Frante, Apaah, Nkrampo, Adiembra and Asubuasu, also employ nurse midwives who deliver the babies of poor villagers.

Involvement of the local community members is a crucial part in the founding of these clinics. For the community to take ownership of the clinics so that it becomes their clinic, they donate the land for the clinic and help build the clinic structure.

Evangelism

It had taken more than an hour over narrow, pitted roads to get to the village. When the Luke Society staff arrived it was dark, and the people were already gathered. We could hear them worshiping as we drove up. In the light of lanterns, a line of women danced before God, waving white handkerchiefs in the air, while men clapped and played drums. This was the newly planted church of Nyinasu, already 200 strong. It is one of 24 new churches planted through the work of Society staff in the last five years.

The Luke Society's approach to evangelism is two-pronged, utilizing both major crusades and church planting. Through the four to five day crusades, the goal is to unite existing Christian churches, reviving them and causing them to work together to take their towns for Jesus. Baptisms are held on Sundays for new believers, who are then encouraged to choose a local church in which to worship. Because many of those who come to Christ have been involved in idol worship, the crusades include deliverance sessions to bind spirits, cast out demons and set people free from satanic and ancestral covenants. In this freedom, they can engage in new covenants in God through Christ.

The second part of the two-pronged approach to evangelism is church planting. New churches are planted in unreached villages, such as the village of Dauda.

Bumping over the rutted road at dusk, a number of us from the Luke Society, accompanied by several believers from Kasei and Amantin, are on our way to the primarily Muslim village of Dauda. Bringing with us the Jesus film in the Twi language and our Bibles, we are prepared to call community members to follow Christ. We have already been praying and fasting for the past week for this crusade and have conducted several all-night prayer vigils.

Arriving in Dauda, we make our way through the village, announcing our presence with a portable public address system. We go first to the house of the village chief chairman to greet him and his assemblymen. This shows respect for the leadership. After this, we set up the projector and lights.

Soon a tractor arrives pulling a trailer full of loudly singing Christians. These are the believers from the church of Amantin, a village not far away. They have come to help plant the new church in Dauda. Shouting greetings, they leap from the trailer, unload benches and drums which they have hauled from their own church and quickly set up. Within a few minutes, a worship service is in full swing. At first the people from Dauda observe curiously. But when the Christian women begin dancing, some women from Dauda join in.

That night, 38 adults and about 75 children become Christians. The seed of a new church has been planted. Before we leave the village that night, a lay leader from Amantin is appointed to help guide the new church.

To promote the sustainability of these new churches and to ensure that they are discipled by mature believers, committed members from previously planted churches are called upon to disciple the new believers. They will also receive regular visits from Luke Society staff.

Prayer, fasting, good planning and the participation of staff members and local church leaders are the keys to the high rates of growth in church membership seen through these evangelistic efforts. Many churches in the area join our staff in round-the-clock prayer and fasting vigils before beginning a new crusade or a new church planting effort.

Income generation

Only a small portion of Kasei's 30-acre compound is occupied by buildings. The rest is under cultivation. Corn, cowpeas, plantain, pineapples and other fruit occupy a large part of the land. Other parts are grazed by sheep and goats. Plans are under way for the introduction of cattle.

The Luke Society was granted a permanent home in Ghana when the Kasei chief, who wanted to support the work, gave the deed to the land on which the Society's facilities are constructed. Attempting to make wise use of the land, we offered employment to some of Kasei's people on the small farm. Besides helping to feed the staff members and recovering patients, the people sell produce and the earnings are put back into the Luke Society's ministry. A portion of these earnings is tithed into other ministries. Those supported in this way include a fatherless boy whose school fees are being paid, a Liberian refugee who is being sent to college and a young Ghanaian Christian who is being sent to seminary. Funds have also been used to rebuild the Anglican schools in Kasei and several church buildings, all of which had fallen into disrepair.

Farming cooperatives, our second major income-generating project, are in their initial stages. One of Ghana's wealthiest businessmen, a deeply committed Christian, recently donated to the Luke Society 2,000 acres in Ejura, one of Kasei's neighboring villages. The land was donated with the understanding that all of the proceeds would be put back into winning souls. A major benefit to the land is that there are six silos there.

The goal of the farming cooperatives is to offer community members a way of generating their own income. This will empower them to have better lives and will also teach them to work together. In turn, the income of our rural clinics will increase because more patients will be able to pay for the services offered. This in turn will allow us to expand our work to more areas. The leader of the cooperative farming plan is Joseph Mintah, who also serves as the evangelism coordinator. Joseph brings with him 25 years of experience in working with cooperatives.

The cooperative program will start small, to educate the farmers in the principles behind successful cooperatives before they make a commitment to join the cooperative. The farmers will then be provided with credits to buy farming implements to farm their own fields and a field that is farmed jointly. When harvests come in, produce will be sold through the cooperative. Because of the silos, crops can be stored until market prices are good and farmers can get a good return. This is very important because many farmers are too poor to store their crops, and often have to sell them when prices are low.

The other side of the farming cooperative will be the cooperative credit union. The money earned by these farmers will be invested in the credit union, which will help other villagers to start small businesses.

The groundwork has been laid for the cooperative and the credit union by receiving the approval of the village chiefs for their implementation. The next step is to approach each village and do study groups to see which farmers wish to join the cooperative, and how the cooperative should be implemented in each location. A network of relationships between Luke Society staff and village members already exists.

Collaborative links

Since many of the ministries, government and nongovernmental organizations and local leaders are working to achieve common goals within Ghana, building supportive relationships with these groups has been a key objective of the Luke Society's work.

For example, Luke Society staff worked to gain the support of the district assembly in the Ashanti region. This support has proven critical because it provides a foundation with which to present the work to village leaders before starting new projects. Relationships with these village leaders have in turn been helpful to our work, because these leaders have often been willing to supply the premises on which to build a health clinic or church.

UNICEF has provided us with assistance in the form of medical supplies and health education materials. We have also partnered with various organizations like World Vision, in projects such as the founding of Christian schools and the provision of clean water to communities through protected wells. As we begin work on setting up credit unions, we have partnered with Sinapi Aba, a Ghanaian micro-enterprise organization, and Opportunity International. I feel strongly that these constructive partnering relationships have been built by the grace of God, formed over the span of many years as staff have interacted with leaders in various settings.

Other key principles we follow in the course of the work include:

1. Recruit staff from the local communities. Staff recruited from outside these communities should live within the communities whenever possible.

2. If funding organizations are willing to provide funds for needs that exist within communities, we will work with them. If what they offer is not needed within the communities, we will not work with them. We will not create programs just because funds exist.

3. We will not work with organizations that will not permit us to share the gospel. We do not want our work to become diluted. If someone wants to offer funding but does not want us to preach the gospel, we will not work with them. We will not compromise in this area, and we believe that God will take care of our needs as we seek to honor him.

4. People need both physical care and release from spiritual bondage to fully become the people that God intends them to be.

Results of the program

One case that demonstrates both spiritual and social change is that of Rebecca Osei, a Luke Society worker at the Kasei compound, who is now a Christian. Rebecca described her life this way: "I was a fetish priestess. The spirits would come upon me when I would carry a bucket of water on my head containing the fetish. When the spirit would come upon me I would no longer be in conscious life." Rebecca said she had a talisman which, when she

101

touched it to water and then to her eye, caused her to vanish. After accepting Christ and turning from unhealthy practices, however, she can now assist in the process of healing for others who come to the clinic.

Another case of changed lives is that of Jackson and his family, also from Kasei. Jackson has a large family of seven children. He is a committed elder in the church, but was unable to produce enough food to feed himself and his family. They lived in a poorly constructed home. With credit inputs he received from the Luke Society, he increased his land tillage and farm products several times. He now has his own modest home, and his children are clothed and can now attend school.

Asubuasu village represents the changes experienced by many of the villages in which we have worked. Asubuasu is located in a remote part of the Ashanti province—so remote that it is inaccessible even by tractor during the rainy season. There was no church there and the village chief is a fetish priest who strongly opposes Christianity.

We first entered this village five years ago. There was no potable water, the only school was located in a dilapidated thatched grass house and there was very poor environmental sanitation. We introduced our program to the villagers on several occasions, and the chief openly opposed our presence, especially opposing the construction of a Christian church in the town.

Our strategy in working with this village was to join regularly in prayer for the villagers, to engage in an educational process with community members and leaders and to spend time in the community, thereby establishing a constant presence there. These efforts bore fruit, and now the village is transformed through having potable water, a new school, a thriving church and a health clinic.

Process of people coming to know Christ

One of the exciting cases we have seen of someone coming to the Lord through our ministry is the case of Peter. Peter was the highest-ranking government official in the county in which the Luke Society's central clinic is located. This case demonstrates how traditional forms of worship can prevent leaders from performing effectively and from being models for other community members to follow.

Peter walked into the clinic's consulting room one day, followed by other officials who looked worried and hopeless. He asked to meet with me and when the two of us were alone in the room, Peter began to cry, saying he could no longer continue with his work or live in the town. Although there were no signs of physical illness, Peter described several days of insomnia, inability to eat, fear of his workplace and inability to live in his official residence. Peter said that he did not go to church and neither had he ever received Christ. He also said, however, that three years earlier he had consulted with three major fetish-*juju* powers, who had each given him a special item for protection.

As I used biblical passages to explain the need for repentance and surrender to Christ as Lord, Peter accepted Christ and renounced all fetish use by burning his fetish objects. After much prayer and ministration, he was baptized by water and the Holy Spirit. Peter has resumed his normal duties, continued in discipleship and is now a member of parliament and a very active witness to Christ among government circles.

Another exciting case is that of Emma. Emma traveled nearly 60 miles (a journey of three hours) for his hernia operation. He accepted Christ on the operating table after hearing the gospel for the first time. He renounced his fetish practices and is now a missionary to his own people and has helped plant three churches.

Along with individual conversions, many people come to know Christ as the gospel is presented to their village during Luke Society evangelistic crusades and church planting efforts. All Luke Society members are involved in sharing the gospel, whether it is through their participation in crusades or as they share their personal testimony during their daily interaction with patients and community members who become involved in our work.

We also encourage those who become Christians through our outreach work to join us in proclaiming the gospel to new communities. We are currently looking for effective ways to build leaders among new converts.

Evaluation of the program

As we move forward in our work, we would like to make the following improvements:

1. Find new ways to train more local community members to lead both the community health outreaches and the newly planted churches. One of the major obstacles we have faced is a lack of leaders among new converts to Christianity.
2. Improve our planning and prioritizing to increase effectiveness and use our human and financial resources wisely.
3. Increase the number of linkages with other agencies to meet the needs of more people in Ashanti Province. We need discernment to determine where best to spend our staff's time and energies.
4. Increase the amount of time spent in prayer and preparation before an evangelistic outreach to increase the effectiveness of the ministry and improve results.
5. Increase the effectiveness of our recruitment practices. Finding qualified health personnel who share the vision has been a major barrier to the expansion of our work.

Challenges we face in our work

1. Finding supplies at an affordable cost.
2. Lack of infrastructure within the region (roads, regular electricity, transportation, other health centers and specialists for referral.)
3. Spiritual warfare encountered from the fetish priests and wizards.
4. Lack of seed capital for the income generation and other projects.

We praise the Lord for his great hand of blessing on this ministry and pray that he will enable us to be even more effective in helping to build his kingdom.

8

Holistic ministry in large-scale relief, Mozambique

Tomas Valoi

W orld Vision Mozambique is a large-scale relief program, involving components of agriculture, commodities distribution and health care. With the coming of peace in the country, the program is moving out of its relief phase and into rehabilitation and development.

When World Vision (WV) began its work in Mozambique in 1984, the country was in the midst of one of the most brutal and destructive civil wars ever documented. After 500 years of Portuguese rule, which did little to advance the Mozambicans in terms of skills and education, a ten-year war of liberation was won by Frelimo (Mozambican Liberation Front), a Mozambican Marxist-socialist movement, which led to the country's independence in 1975.

During this time, the vast majority of educated, skilled individuals fled the country. Though the new Frelimo government tried to compensate with education and training programs, their efforts were soon undermined by a guerilla resistance movement called Renamo (Mozambican National Resistance). From its inception, Renamo's mandate was not to attack military targets or well-defended cities, but to sabotage the country's infrastructure and to destroy the rural economy. Renamo's soldiers came largely from the rural population. Thousands of men, women and children were killed or kidnapped during Renamo raids, and millions were driven from their homelands, unable to farm or support themselves.

When WV entered Mozambique, large pockets of isolated populations were in severe famine conditions or already dying of malnutrition. These conditions were compounded by the severe drought that affected many of the provinces in the years before 1992.

Renamo's successful campaign to destabilize the country meant that most of the country's infrastructure was in ruins. For example, in Manica Province, which is representative of the nine other provinces in Mozambique, 208 of the 390 primary schools had been destroyed or had no infrastructure while 114 of them required major rehabilitation. Of the existing 141 health clinics, 48 were destroyed and 59 were in need of major rehabilitation. Most of the boreholes in rural areas had been destroyed due to sabotage or lack of maintenance, and villagers frequently walked up to 50 kilometers in search of water. Agricultural production was seriously affected by the concentration of people in Frelimo-defended suburban zones, and the inaccessibility, due to fighting and land mines, of most rural areas. Even clothing was difficult to come by and tree bark served as covering for many.

In Sofala Province, as of October 1992 when Frelimo and Renamo had signed a peace accord, it was estimated that three-quarters of the major roads, excluding the two national highways, were inaccessible for vehicles because of mines, destroyed bridges and unpassable road surfaces. This was one of the factors that compounded the difficulty of providing relief commodities to isolated populations, as the goods had to be flown in or brought in through convoy.

The severity of this structural devastation does not even compare with the extreme suffering inflicted emotionally, mentally and physically on the lives of the country's citizens, who experienced torture, murder of loved ones, kidnapping of their children to serve as soldiers and the destruction of their homes and property. During the 17-year civil war between the country's independence in 1975 and the peace accord of 1992, more than one million people died in

106

war-related deaths, more than four million were displaced within the country and almost two million fled to the neighboring countries of Malawi, South Africa, Swaziland, Tanzania and Zimbabwe.

When you look at the country in terms of its Christian witness, the church is expanding rapidly. After having been active in churches in Malawian camps, one of the first things many former refugees want to do upon returning to Mozambique is build a church for their home community. According to a 1994 survey, the number of Christians in the country is growing at a rate of 7.6 percent, while the population growth rate is 2.7 percent.

Aside from being the poorest country in the world, Mozambique has the largest number of unreached people groups in Africa south of the equator. These groups are located primarily in the northern provinces. In southern Mozambique, however, the Protestant Church has been a strong and active force since the late 1800s, mainly because Mozambican migrants to South Africa returned to Mozambique with the desire to plant Protestant churches in their own country. For example, the Presbyterian Church of Mozambique is the Protestant denomination with the second largest number of congregations in the country. Mozambican Tsonga migrants to South Africa, having been converted to Christianity during their time there, returned to Mozambique and established the Presbyterian church in their home country in 1881. It was only later, at the request of these Tsonga missionaries, that the Swiss Mission, the first Protestant mission to arrive in the country, was invited to Mozambique.

It is difficult to make cultural generalizations within Mozambique because of the large number of people groups living within the country. In a number of the communities where WV works, however, one of the traditional cultural-religious practices affecting Christian practice and behavior is ancestor worship. Many people believe that ancestral spirits are very closely involved in people's day-to-day lives and can exercise real powers, for good or evil. Many times those belonging to Christian churches will "hedge their bets" by constructing a shelter in their yard for their ancestors and keeping the shelter clean and well stocked. Or they will pray to

God, but will continue as well to pray to their ancestors in times of urgent need, such as an illness in the family.

In 1984, during the first years of WV's work within Mozambique, the Frelimo government's policy was to promote Marxism and to strongly discourage participation in church activities. The government's stand softened steadily over the years, however, and was lifted completely in late 1990, when President Chissano declared the governing structures of Mozambique to be democratic.

Description of the holistic ministry program

World Vision's interventions began with relief food aid in areas selected by the government of Mozambique. This was soon followed by seed and tool distributions to food aid recipients and, in 1988, emergency and primary health care programs. Though WV's program interventions in relief were intended to be temporary and quickly followed up with rehabilitation and development efforts, this intent was undermined by the ongoing civil war. Even after the peace accord was signed in 1992, the high numbers of returning refugees pushed to the breaking point the support systems WV had set up.

World Vision Mozambique's three main programs are commodities, health and agriculture. A chart for fiscal year 1994 showing detailed program statistics in each of these areas is included at the end of this chapter. Through the commodities program, WV has supplied food and non-food items to hundreds of thousands of people throughout the country, making it the largest distributor of food commodities within Mozambique. Up to June 1994, it is estimated that WV had delivered 106,458 metric tons of commodities. As peace has held and the situation for many has grown less desperate, WV has moved from strictly relief aid into the rehabilitation phase, and has begun food- or cash-for-work projects to rehabilitate or construct schools, health clinics, agricultural posts, roads and agricultural irrigation systems. Many villagers have been employed through the new jobs these projects have created.

The agricultural program, initiated in 1986, focuses largely on the distribution of agricultural seeds and hand tools to displaced families who have suffered severe disruption to their farming systems because of the civil war. In addition, technical agricultural support is provided to enhance the farmers' ability to generate maximum outputs from their crops.

The health program, initiated in 1988, has had the following major components:

1. Immunization of infants, children and women of childbearing age
2. Growth monitoring and nutritional surveillance
3. Prenatal, natal and postpartum care for mothers
4. Diarrhea and malaria prevention
5. Water and sanitation activities and other preventive education

Program activities have expanded to include rehabilitation and even developmental components such as STD-HIV (sexually transmitted diseases-human immunodeficiency virus) prevention, child spacing and family planning, equipping of health posts and health staff training.

In both the agricultural and health programs, WV cooperates closely with the government ministries of agriculture and health. Part of our strategy is to build the technical capacity of staff in these ministries to promote the sustainability of the work.

It is relevant at this point to discuss funding sources for WV's work in Mozambique. The Mozambique program is the largest of WV's programs around the world. Due to the catastrophic nature of the events in Mozambique, the needs were greater than what the private sector could fund, and WV made the decision to work mainly through government funds. The program budget expanded from US$20 million in 1992 to US$80 million in 1994. Eighty-seven percent of this funding is from government donors. Along with the tremendous opportunities made possible by such large amounts of funding have come restrictions in terms of Christian witness.

The initial funding for WV's Mozambique program came from the government of Holland. It was difficult to gain funding from the U.S. because this was during the cold war and the Mozambican government was Marxist. Over time, however, as donor governments saw the effectiveness of WV's work, willingness to fund these activities increased. By September 1994, 68 percent of the funding for WV's work came from six donor governments, 20 percent from five UN agencies and the European Community and the remaining 13 percent from private donations.

Until 1990, due to Mozambican government policy and the policies of various governments funding WV's work, Christian witness came about through the staff's informal contacts with program beneficiaries, staff devotions, and staff members' personal church work, prayer and Bible study after hours. These efforts were not part of a strategy, but were the spontaneous results of staff efforts.

In 1990, however, WV was able to draw on funds from private donors interested in supporting evangelism and church growth in Mozambique. Though WV's government-funded relief programs prohibited formal Christian activities of any sort, a new operational program called church relations was started, headed by Tanya Brenneman, a former WV employee. The purpose of the program was to support the churches and other Christian institutions, especially in their work among displaced and drought-affected populations. WV was able to contribute to the expansion of Scripture Union's ministry—headed by Guilherme Nhanale Jr., who had also worked for WV—to all 10 provincial capitals throughout the country. This in turn led to increased Bible reading and biblical seminars throughout the country. Through the provision of funds to Scripture Union, Overseas Crusades Ministries and other Christian institutions, the following activities have been carried out in cooperation with WV:

1. Training of pastors and church leaders through seminars, enabling them to better serve their churches and to promote a clear and practical understanding of the gospel to their communities;
2. Promotion of Bible reading and Bible study among church leaders, youth and other believers;
3. Distribution in all provinces of Portuguese and native lan-

guage literature such as Bibles, tracts, Bible study materials and hymnals;

4. Promotion of Christian growth and leadership through Bible correspondence classes; and
5. Provision of training and materials for Sunday school teachers and youth group leaders in all provinces.

As WV is moving from the emergency phase to the rehabilitation and reconstruction phase, the church relations project is also seeking new ways by which it can improve its assistance to churches. During this period training, literature distribution and research of the basic needs of the churches will continue.

Key principles that we will continue to work by include:

1. Supporting, rather than duplicating, the work of the able-bodied church and parachurch organizations existing throughout Mozambique through funding support and training.
2. Focusing on the importance of building leadership capacity among pastors and other church leaders.
3. Promoting Bible study and daily Bible reading to train all believers in an understanding of the Christian faith.
4. Making the gospel accessible to as many people as possible through literature distribution.
5. Training a new generation of Christian leaders through supporting Sunday school classes and youth training.

As we have worked in cooperation with local churches throughout the country, the churches themselves have played a key role. They have contributed to the various programs by providing trainers, sending members of their congregations to participate in WV-funded seminars and helping in the preparation of Bible booklets and Bible distributions.

The restrictions placed by donor governments on Christian witness give rise to the question of how a Christian agency can carry out its holistic mandate in the face of such restrictions. In September 1994, WV's international office carried out a review with a primary objective of determining what it means to offer an effective

Christian witness in a relief context where government funding is used. In preparation for that review, a survey was carried out among a number of WV staff in Mozambique to determine what Christian witness activities staff were involved in during "off hours" and the impact of these activities throughout the country. The information that follows was gathered during the course of the survey and the review.

Results of the program

As a result of WV's programs in Mozambique, two and-a-half million people are receiving food and assistance to enable them to begin the process of resettling into their normal lives. WV programs have allowed thousands of Mozambicans to begin planting on time to harvest their first crops after returning to their home communities. Thousands of others have been trained in health care. Others have had the lives of their children saved in WV feeding centers. For specific numbers during 1994, see the program overview and history at the end of the chapter.

Informal Christian witness opportunities have their greatest impact on program beneficiaries in the health program, where more time is spent with the people than in the commodities or agriculture programs. The health team members based in the city of Quelimane and working throughout the Zambezia Province actively and creatively offer their Christian testimony in a way that has made a significant and measurable impact. The director of health countrywide opens all meetings with nurses and health assistants with prayer. All health seminars with the government's Ministry of Health begin with devotions and the basic salvation message is often shared. It was at one of these seminars that 25 of the 40 nurses attending the seminar gave their lives to Christ.

The following stories represent physical and spiritual healings as a result of the testimony and prayers of WV staff members.

One village woman named Eusebia was delivered from a spirit who kept her from responding to her name. Whenever someone used her real name instead of the spirit's name, Eusebia would fall to the ground, unconscious. This particular name spirit is a well known spirit in the Zambezia Province. Eusebia and her family of four gave their lives to Christ after hearing the gospel preached by a WV health staff member.

Another woman was delivered from a spirit that did not allow her to eat meat. She ate meat for the first time in many years after confessing Christ as Lord and receiving prayer for deliverance.

In a village where the health team was working, they noticed that there was poor receptivity to building latrines. They discovered that this was because the key leaders in that community were drinking and unable to take responsibility for the improvement of their village. The WV staff member took the opportunity to speak with these leaders about their lifestyle and about what the Bible says about life after death. All 10 of these men gave their lives to Christ. A church was planted with 58 members in the community, and the men no longer drink.

In the village of Maria Rua, the health staff member brought an evangelist with him as he met with village leaders about water and sanitation. As a result, a new church with 78 members was planted.

In summary, 14 new churches with 847 members were started in Tete, Zambezia and Sofala provinces as a direct result of the preaching and praying by WV staff during their free hours or evangelists preaching in the communities at the invitation of WV staff. Out of these churches have come an additional 12 churches with a total of 655 members. All of these churches are in rural areas. The English-speaking church in Maputo has grown from a congregation of 50 to 200. WV staff believe this is due in part to the organization and proper running of the steering committee in which they participate.

Process of people coming to know Christ

Throughout Mozambique, WV staff are involved in many diverse Christian outreach endeavors. What follows is a sampling of these activities. These activities are being carried out by national and expatriate staff in all departments, including commodities, health, agriculture and administration.

As the list shows, although funding requirements restrict Christian witness activities during work hours, there is still a wide range of activities that can be carried out during non-work hours. Relief funding has allowed many Christians to be placed in strategic areas throughout the country where the need to hear the gospel is great. Personal initiative coupled with the strength of the Lord has allowed staff to respond to the need.

❖ Serving as chair of the steering committee for the international church in Maputo
❖ Leading Bible studies in their homes
❖ Fasting and praying weekly for the country and WV's work
❖ Leading devotions at the start of health seminars with Ministry of Health nurses
❖ Preaching in the rural churches
❖ Serving as president of the Gideons International
❖ Leading a Christian student organization that meets weekly
❖ Serving as vice president of the planning commission for an evangelical crusade to the city of Quelimane
❖ Visiting and mobilizing local churches over the weekends
❖ Serving as assistant to the pastor of a Baptist church
❖ Preaching the gospel in project areas and distributing Bibles
❖ Planting new churches
❖ Teaching Bible stories at an orphanage for street children
❖ Sharing the faith with Renamo soldiers undergoing demobilization
❖ Inviting evangelists to preach in project areas
❖ Praying with patients in the feeding centers

As a direct result of the above activities, 127 people have given their lives to Christ. This includes 30 health assistants from Renamo-controlled areas who were working in cooperation with WV and 25 emergency health nurses from the Ministry of Health.

Evaluation of the program

The question of how to express Christian witness in a program funded largely through restrictive government funding is one that deserves consideration. Since different donor governments have different rules in terms of the amount and type of witness they allow, it would help staff to understand the requirements of the donor government funding their particular project. That way, rather than assuming that the strictest requirements apply, staff could adjust their behavior to match the funding requirements.

One of the health staff members said they would like to see greater freedom in exercising their faith along with their professional abilities. This staff member feels people would benefit greatly if spiritual, as well as physical, needs could be met. He sees hundreds of villagers who are benefitting from WV health care, but who still carry charms for protection against disease around their necks. He feels there is much to be done spiritually to deliver people from the forces of darkness, and that this would in turn allow people to better care for themselves physically as well.

There should be communication structures set in place that would promote cooperation between local churches and WV projects. WV should also solicit more cooperation from the churches in terms of project activities. For example, one of the staff in the commodities program suggested that churches could speak to the communities about why WV is involved in assistance programs throughout the country. Church members could assist in the distributions or provide transportation to those who live far away from distribution sites and need to take food back to their homes.

A staff member in the health program also suggested more cooperation with churches. He suggested that WV use churches to mobilize communities for vaccination programs in the villages. Also, AIDS teaching could be done within the churches with church members, who are respected within the rural communities, doing the teaching.

A recommendation made by the WV international office staff members who performed the review was to integrate the Christian witness strategy into the other programs (commodities, health and agriculture) and invest the same level of professionalism in the Christian witness program as is invested in the other programs throughout the country. A further recommendation was to develop a specific strategy to raise private donor funds for the Christian witness-church relations program. While funds for the relief program have increased fourfold during the past couple of years, the church relations project budget was cut in half in 1994 due to the difficulty of raising funds for the program.

One of the serious obstacles faced by staff is that, with the urgent nature of the work in a life-or-death emergency relief situation, the work is physically and emotionally exhausting, and little energy remains for community and church activities. This situation is slowly changing as WV moves out of its relief phase, but the mentality is one that takes time to overcome.

Other obstacles include:

❖ Road conditions throughout the country and the lack of public and personal means of transportation in the rural areas adds to the difficulty of carrying out programs;

❖ The many Muslims and Hindus living in the northern areas of Mozambique has made it more difficult for Christianity to be accepted in these communities;

❖ Lack of leadership training among the churches has slowed WV's ability to effectively partner with them, making training a preliminary step toward meaningful cooperation.

As we consider the obstacles and the improvements to the work that can and will be made, we are thankful to be in a place within the country where we can make a significant contribution to the rebuilding of the nation. It is a time of hope and a time of turning for Mozambique, and we believe that the Lord has placed us here to build his kingdom so that his name will be glorified.

REFERENCES

Andrews, Theresa and Tomas Valoi. "Christian Witness Interview Results." World Vision Mozambique.

Newitt, Malyn. 1993. *A History of Mozambique*. Indiana University Press.

Office for Humanitarian Assistance Coordination. "Report on the Consolidated Humanitarian Assistance Programme 1992-1994."

Testimony given by a Catholic Maryknoll Sister to the U.S. Senate Subcommittee on Africa. The Sister was a long-term development worker in Africa and in Mozambique, and her testimonry focused on Mozambique.

Van Butselaar, Jan. *Fundadores da Igreja Presbiteriana de Mocambique*. Translated by Francisco da Cruz.

Voorhies, Samuel J. and Jack Fortin. "WV Mozambique Christian Witness Review Final Report." World Vision International.

Appendix 1:
World Vision Mozambique Program Statistics*

Agricultural Recovery Program	Fiscal Year 1994
Ag Paks distributed 93/94 Season Ag Paks purchased 94/95 Season	262,000 300,000
Veg Paks distributed	260,000
D-Paks** distributed	60,000
Tools to be distributed	812,000
Field trials planned	910
Target population/teaching sessions	3,527
Total target beneficiaries (approx.)	1,500,000
Budget commitment	US$16,199,000

Child Survival Program	Fiscal Year 1994
Vaccines to be given to women of childbearing age and children	60,000
Growth monitoring consults	22,000
Pre- and post-natal exams planned	2,300
Participants in teaching sessions	32,000
Latrines to be constructed	300
Feeding centers	9
Total target beneficiaries (approx.)	250,000
Budget commitment	US$3,673,000

Commodities Program	Fiscal Year 1994
Food aid: metric tons (mt) committed	137,412 mt
Cash value of food committed	US$42,237,000
Survival kits to be distributed	38,000
Total target beneficiaries (approx.)	773,800
Budget commitment	US$19,032,000

Emergency Response Program	Fiscal Year 1994
Airlift sites (with feeding centers)	3
Clothing/non-food items to be distributed	50 mt
Emergency airlifts planned	10,400 mt
Total target beneficiaries (approx.)	40,000
Budget commitment	US$4,524,000

Overall Program Statistics	Fiscal Year 1994
Provinces and districts to be served	5 provinces 42 districts
Staff - Mozambican Expatriate	550 52
Budget - Committed Food Value (Gift-In-Kind)	US$43,428,000 US$36,820,000

*Figures represent commitments or allocations for each program area for World Vision fiscal year 1994 (1 October 1993-30 September 1994). These tables were prepared by World Vision Mozambique staff.
** Demobilization kit for soldiers leaving the military to become civilians.

Part two

Reflections

9

Community participation
and holistic development

Samuel J. Voorhies

These cases represent the real life experiences of people trying
to live out their call to the gospel. Theirs is a holistic call to
minister to the whole person, meeting both physical and
spiritual needs (Acts 4:31-37). How do the cases reflect what we
know about effective development practice? How can the practice
of holistic development improve our understanding of what constitutes effective development?

These cases represent significant achievements. More people are
food self-sufficient, healthy, have clean water and access to education. There has been effective "Christian witness"—people have
come to know Christ, others have been delivered from satanic
bondage, new churches have been started, existing churches have
grown and people are sharing their increased resources with needy
neighbors and with the church.

How and why has this happened? What approaches of effective
development were followed in the cases that have led to such successes?

Each case is unique, representing the experience and perspective
of the particular people involved. Yet they have things in common
as well. Are there differences between what the experience of oth-

ers suggests makes for effective development and what the experiences in these cases reveal?

Holistic meanings

Holistic ministry, transformational development, integrated development, holistic community-based sustainable development—these are all phrases that attempt to capture and describe approaches to working with people, usually in communities, to facilitate change. These approaches seek to facilitate changes in peoples' attitudes, fundamental values, beliefs and behavior; changes to improve the quality of life of the people involved, from agricultural practice to sexual behavior to a person's view and practice of religion.

To some, a holistic approach means designing a development program so that it deals with the whole community. It is an integrated approach looking at various economic and social aspects of the community's development. To others the concept of holism includes addressing development issues related to the whole person's mind, body and spirit. And, as suggested in the preparation for the writing of these case studies, "holistic ministry" can refer to programs where "relief and development efforts have led to the creation of new churches or the expansion of existing churches."

The Africa Consultation gathered to discuss cases of "effective" holistic ministry, for "the purpose of identifying lessons learned and principles employed, in order to assist others engaged in similar ministries." The cases in this book document examples of effective development principles. My reflections on these cases will seek to identify lessons and principles from the perspective of development theory and practice, focusing especially on community participation. (See the references section at the end of this chapter for additional holistic ministry resources.)

Effective development

"More and more effective development is being understood as the development of indigenous cultures and as a process of change rather than a specific level of achievement," concluded a consultation between churches and the Canadian International Development Agency (Geest 1993). Drawing from the experience of Canadian-funded programs, the consultation went on to suggest that the role and views of local people are not only important to local ownership but to achieving effective, sustainable development.

Based on research and experience, a broad consensus now exists on basic approaches that lead to effective development. These approaches include the following.

- ❖ Community participation, empowerment, ownership and sustainability;
- ❖ An integrated or holistic approach;
- ❖ The respect for and continuity of local culture; and
- ❖ A networking and partnership approach between agencies and the local community.

We see elements of all these approaches in our case studies. Of these approaches, two primary areas have been found to be the most critical for achieving effective development. These are the concepts of *community participation* and *sustainability*.

In this chapter I have chosen to focus primarily on community participation as a cornerstone of effective development. Without appropriate participation there will not be ownership. Without ownership there is little hope of achieving sustainability. I suggest that this is relevant whether the development activity is agriculture, health or church planting.

"Development is participation." Many development practitioners and researchers argue that participation is the essence of development. Also, the concept and practice of participation in overseas development projects has increasingly become a central policy issue for both government and private aid agencies as a necessary ingredient for long-term sustainable results (Voorhies 1990, 1993).

In Africa, the concept of self-participatory development has been popular for many years in certain countries, especially in Tanzania. Taking a decentralized approach, this view moves the focus of development control and effort from the national government and the capital to the rural village and homestead (Bragg 1983; Nyerere

1976). In this approach, some kind of community structure at the local level takes primary responsibility for deciding what type of development is needed, planning how to achieve local development goals, pursuing the required internal and external government and nongovernment sources, and actually carrying out the development activities (Rogers 1976).

Development participation

It is important to define what we mean by the term "participation," and to identify the conceptual parameters for examining this issue. There are many ways to define and analyze the concept of local participation in development. I offer several prominent perspectives here and draw comparisons with the experiences represented in the case studies.

While the value of participation has generally been affirmed, it is also important to recognize that participation alone does not guarantee development success. "The value of participation depends upon what kind it is, under what circumstances it is taking place and by and for whom," concluded a four-year study of rural development participation experience and literature (Uphoff 1979:281).

In an effort to provide a conceptual framework for considering the issues of development participation, Uphoff and his colleagues define participation as a descriptive term rather than as a single phenomenon, denoting, "the involvement of a significant number of persons in situations or actions which enhance their well-being, e.g., their income, security or self esteem" (Uphoff 1979:4). While this definition is a very general one, perhaps, as Norman T. Uphoff (1979) suggests, it captures the range of things most people refer to when discussing the concept in the abstract.

From an analytical point of view, Uphoff suggests considering participation in terms of three dimensions. These include: "(1) *What kind* of participation is under consideration? (2) *Who* is participating in it? and (3) *How* is participation occurring? Moreover, it is necessary to consider closely the *context* in which participation is occurring or intended to occur" (1979:5).

126

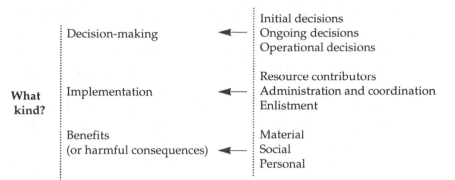

**What
kind?**

Decision-making   ◄——   Initial decisions
                                          Ongoing decisions
                                          Operational decisions

Implementation   ◄——   Resource contributors
                                          Administration and coordination
                                          Enlistment

Benefits   Material
(or harmful consequences)   ◄——   Social
                                          Personal

Evaluation

Who?

Local residents   Characteristics
                                          Age
                                          Sex
Local leaders   Family status
                                          Education
Government personnel   Social divisions
                                          Income level
Foreign personnel   Length of residence
                                          Land tenure status

How?

Basis of participation   < Impetus
                                          < Incentives
Form of participation   < Organization
                                          < Direct-Indirect
Extent of participation   < Time involved
                                          < Range of activities
Effect of participation   < Empowerment
                                          < Interactions

**Figure 9.1. Basic framework for describing and analyzing rural
development participation (Source: Cohen and Uphoff 1980:219).**

These dimensions of participation concern *what kind* of participation is taking place, the *sets* of persons involved in the participatory process and the specific *characteristics* of that process. By looking at the context of participation, one can see the relationship between the development project's characteristics and the pattern of actual participation that emerges (Uphoff 1979).

The dimensions of participation are further delineated by providing specific elements under each of the above dimensions. These may be summarized by Figure 9.1 on page 127.

A quick analysis of what kind of participation is occurring, by whom and in what ways, will provide an overall picture to determine where there might be gaps or weaknesses in a particular program approach. This framework might be applied to analyze participation in an agricultural or health program as well as in a program for planting and establishing a church.

Another source, D. D. Gow and J. VanSant (1983b), suggests participation means much more than project staff simply discussing plans with local people, but that it means "systematic local autonomy" (p. 47). This involves communities in the process of discovering the possibilities of exercising choice and becoming capable of managing their own development.

In conducting a review of evaluations of some 75 USAID-funded projects, Judith Tendler (1982:15) suggested that we may view participatory decision-making in private voluntary organization (PVO) experience in three categories. These were: (1)"genuine representative participation where 'the poorest groups are fully represented in decision-making'"; (2) "top-down 'sensitive,'" where the PVO consults with those who will benefit from the project but dominates service delivery decisions; and (3) "local elite decision-making" that allows for local tailoring of projects by a limited few. Tendler submitted that this last category really represented decentralized rather than participatory project management.

From these definitions our cases appear to represent a range of different types of participation (see Table 9.1 on page 129).

Case Studies	Type of Participation	Participation Activities
• World Vision Ethiopia • Rushinga Cattle • Zambuko Trust	*Genuine Representative Participation*: Participation in all areas of the development process.	• Planning • Needs analysis and resource identification • Decision-making • Implementation • Management • Monitoring • Evaluation
• Food for the Hungry-Agriculture • Food for the Hungry-AIDS • The Luke Society	*Top-Down Sensitive*: Community members are consulted but primarily participate through resource contribution, such as labor or material.	• Burning bricks • Hauling sand • Service delivery committees
• Chidamoyo AIDS • World Vision Mozambique	*Decentralized*: Participation occurs primarily as beneficiaries receive goods and services from the project activities, which are controlled and delivered by outsiders or "local elites."	• AIDS care • Skills training • Medical services • Relief assistance

Table 9.1. Aspects of participation observed in the cases

Guidelines and principles for facilitating participation

The knowledge and experience that have accumulated over the last 30 years offer a set of operating guidelines on how to best achieve effective participation (Gow and VanSant 1983b). The experiences in our cases affirm these guidelines. These ideas may be helpful since some of the cases are still moving toward sustainable forms of community participation.

1. *Community involvement in assessing needs and planning.* People organize best around problems they consider most important. Community participation in assessing needs and in planning development initiatives is essential for an effective local response to such initiatives.

Our cases report that it was best to identify and start with community strengths. Even in the poorest communities there was the capacity to contribute and be an active participant in the development process (Food for the Hungry International [FHI] agriculture and AIDS projects, Rushinga cattle project). Where projects began with the ideas of the local people instead of those imposed by the outside agency, there was greater impact.

Handouts lead to dependency, not self-respect or self-reliance. As one case study reflected, next time the project staff would reduce the number of handouts. No matter how poor or desperate the situation, focus on what people can do for themselves, however little that may be. Starting with the ideas and resources of the people also communicates respect for them; it puts the outside facilitator in a learning posture. The outsider becomes dependent on the community members, not the other way around.

We must recognize that local people make rational decisions in the context of their own environment and circumstances. Their willingness to adopt new practices or technologies depends on their assessment of risks and possible rewards, which are based on very pragmatic considerations that outsiders frequently misunderstand. Their involvement in the initial planning can identify information from their perspective that the outsider cannot easily observe.

Initially people were not willing to get involved in the banana plantation scheme of the FHI agriculture program (see chapter three). The project staff found that "as some farmers began to prosper and develop confidence in our approach, more people wanted to begin farming."

2. *Start small*. A project should start small, with simple activities that respond to the needs and capabilities of the local situation. In many situations where outsiders have initiated the intervention, it was necessary to provide an incentive for people to see the benefit of participating. These initial activities, therefore, should produce results quickly (Garcia-Zamor 1985; Honadle and VanSant 1985; Bryant and White 1984).

Success breeds success. Once a community has a successful experience in helping themselves, they are more likely to try to do more. In the FHI agriculture project, communities went from a successful agricultural program to working together to build a local primary school. Also, in the FHI AIDS program, churches began to initiate their own income-generating projects to help care for AIDS victims.

At least three of the cases reported that they should have gone slower in the beginning, spending more time on building relationships and helping the community to organize and "own" the development process. The Zambuko Trust approach of providing small graduated loans, initially over a short period of time, with training, illustrates this point. As the borrower demonstrates responsibility and success with the "little," the loans are increased. Zambuko Trust increases loans in relationship to a demonstrated, sustainable business.

3. *Resource contribution.* A minimal form of participation involves potential beneficiaries making a resource commitment to the project completion (Bryant and White 1984; Uphoff 1979). No community is too poor to contribute something. Voluntary local investment of labor, time, material and money in a project is evidence of popular participation and a necessary condition for breaking patterns of paternalism, which reinforce local passivity and dependency.

In most of the cases, some form of local resource contribution was seen as a minimal form of participation. This ranged from burning bricks and hauling sand, to building a local school, and to volunteers forming care groups to look after AIDS victims. People even donated land and helped build clinics. This crucial involvement, the Luke Society program found, resulted in "the community [taking] ownership of the clinics so that it becomes their clinic."

Where people are not willing to participate in this way, it may be necessary to wait until they are ready or to bypass them. In the FHI agriculture program, villages were not willing to participate until they began to see the tangible benefits gained by the neighboring communities who were involved in the program.

4. *Take a process approach.* Facilitating effective participation requires a process approach to project implementation and management. This process approach, in contrast to the blueprint approach,

131

involves a willingness by project staff and beneficiaries to try various alternatives and readjust plans and procedures as necessary to the ongoing demands of the situation. Such an approach means that not only should the aid recipients learn, but that learning occur within the implementing agency as well (Korten 1980; Bryant and White 1984; Garcia-Zamor 1985; Rondinelli 1983).

We can observe a learning process approach in some of the cases, particularly in the Rushinga cattle project. The project was expanded and adjusted as success was experienced and the local people took on more and more responsibility. The program went through three distinct phases—from relief to rehabilitation to development. The role of the implementing agency changed from having control over resources and the implementation of services to that of an adviser and networker for the community. As the community took responsibility for resources, approaches were reconsidered and changed based on the experience.

5. *Communication and project implementation.* Establish a two-way information flow, both formal and informal, between project implementers and potential beneficiaries at the start of the project. This is relevant for initially generating accurate data for planning and project design and, later, for implementation, monitoring and evaluation of project activities (Korten 1984; Honadle and VanSant 1985).

A critical part of the concept of "social learning" is the issue of "embracing error." For open communication to occur, there must be flexibility and a willingness within the implementing agency to accept error and use such feedback to make necessary adjustments. The recognition and communication of error must be rewarded, not punished (Korten 1980; Bryant and White 1984).

Again, we see some evidence of this attitude and approach in the Rushinga cattle project. The cash payback in the loan scheme for cattle was not working. This had to be recognized and an alternative approach devised. The agency was not locked into one approach.

6. *Community organization.* To the greatest extent possible, projects should try to work—formally and informally—with and through community organizations. Local organizations are com-

monly regarded as the most practical and effective means of achieving participation (Bryant and White 1984; Honadle and VanSant 1985).

There is some debate as to whether it is better to use existing local organizations or to create new ones. There are pros and cons to either, depending on the situation. What is most important is using some form of local organization that can: 1) communicate technical information to individuals and break down barriers between groups or individuals; 2) establish economies of scale; 3) adapt project activities to local conditions; 4) marshall local resources; 5) achieve political clout by exercising influence over local administrators and asserting claims on government; 6) sustain project benefits; and 7) coordinate and distribute the benefits of outside assistance.

The cases in this book demonstrate both the use of existing institutional structures, such as church and government, and the establishment of new organizational structures. In several cases, committees were formed or elected to oversee different project interventions in areas such as health and sanitation, reforestation, agriculture, water and education, and flour mill management. In the Rushinga program, formation of a cooperative enabled local control over a loan scheme for cattle, plows and fertilizer.

7. *Local control over benefits.* Through community-based organizations, local control over the amount, quality and distribution of benefits from development activities represents the ultimate confirmation of participation and is directly related to those benefits becoming self-sustaining.

The Rushinga program had started in the form of handouts. After assuming responsibility the local leaders determined to provide material in the form of a loan that could be repaid and then loaned again within the community.

At first the loan scheme involved loan repayment in cash. After evaluating this approach, it was determined that the price of cattle was rising faster than repayment, causing a decline in the total number of cattle that could be purchased. A new approach was agreed upon: to repay the loan by keeping the calf and passing the heifer to the next family in the program. According to the case study, this approach has worked very well. As others in the community—people initially reluctant to participate—saw success, they also made requests for loans.

8. *Power, conflict and accountability*. Participation often opens the door for increased conflict between social groups within a community. Where this potential exists, it is necessary to work toward reconciliation. Power relations within the community and with the community and other official structures, such as the government or the church, must be recognized and dealt with effectively. As leadership for a project or local initiative emerges, those leaders—regardless of their group or origin—must be held accountable to a broad constituency in the community (Uphoff 1979; Chambers 1985).

Do our "Christian programs" facilitate reconciliation, or do they exacerbate conflicts and tensions in the community? If the assistance being provided is done through local Christian churches or institutional structures, are they used as a power base to exercise authority or as a base of service to the community as a whole?

Any agency can provide health service or dig a bore hole. What difference does it make when it is done by Christians? Are people in the case studies coming to Christ because of the benefits they receive from the project and, once those benefits cease, will they turn away?

9. *Capacity building*. Sustaining participation as well as project benefits will often depend on the community's capacity. Building the basic organizational capacity of communities must be an intentional part of the program strategy. This capacity should include the capability to forge links with other organizations, design and continue ways for local residents to participate in decision-making, collect information from local persons for decision-making and develop processes for solving problems and implementing decisions (Gow and VanSant 1983b).

As community capacity increases, the role of the outside agency should change. For example, in the Rushinga cattle project the community has elected leaders to supervise the running of program activities. The role of the external agency changed from that of supervisor to facilitator, networker and consultant. The community is now responsible for making major decisions. The external agency helps to write funding proposals and network the community with potential donors, a good example of capacity building.

Teaching, training and imparting skills was found to be a critical aspect of capacity building in these cases (especially in the FHI agriculture and AIDS projects, Rushinga cattle project, World Vision [WV] Ethiopia's Ansokia program). This training not only involved a technical area, such as a new health practice or cultivation technique, but also training that focused on imparting the skills necessary to build the people's capacity to plan and manage their own development.

"Promoting the managerial capacity of community members and their full involvement in community activities needs more attention and training," was a finding in the Ansokia program case study. The FHI agricultural program found that a "holistic" training approach was important to building capacity. Materials and training were needed in the areas of health and agriculture, as well as in Christian education and spiritual maturity.

As FHI found, the success in the agricultural project resulted in the community forming development committees and organizing their own school. Schools were not the focus of the outside agency, but through a successful self-help experience in agriculture, the community could address a priority need of its own, despite the outside agency's lack of interest in that area.

The church's Christian or spiritual development needs also required training and support resources, just as any other development activity. People cannot be expected to grow in their faith, learn to share their faith and teach Scripture without training and study resources.

From participation to sustainability

At least three of the cases demonstrate, as Judith Tendler suggests, "genuine representative participation where the poorest groups are fully represented in decision-making" (Tendler 1975). Experience suggests that this form of participation is the most likely to lead to sustainable outcomes. Such an approach requires an intentional strategy.

Participation goes beyond self-help to involvement in every aspect of the development process. It also involves planning, including identifying the problems and opportunities as well as local resources. WV Ethiopia found that establishing priorities, making decisions, carrying out activities and monitoring and evaluating progress are all areas where people can be involved.

The WV Ethiopia Ansokia program and the Rushinga cattle project in particular demonstrate that participation must not only include involvement in project activities, such as contributing labor or materials, but must also involve community members in taking full responsibility for and management of the development process. This includes the responsibility and ability for such things as: problem identification; solution and resource identification; planning and organizing; management and accountability; access to local, government and external resources.

This type of participation has the potential to lead to a sustainable program, whose benefits and impact will continue once the donor and external agency have moved on.

Empowerment, not just participation

Participation alone is not enough for a program to be owned and sustained by the local community. Empowerment must occur as well. Restoring hope and self-confidence within the community is often the first step to empowerment. An initial activity of doing something together that an individual could not achieve, such as transforming muddy springs into clean water that is stored and available near one's home, generates confidence and motivation.

Empowerment also involves the "spiritual" dimension. Fear and adherence to local beliefs can prevent the acceptance of the most basic and needed changes. We must recognize and address the power of evil spirits over individuals, as seen in the experience of the Luke Society. Prayer and spiritual discernment become critical tools of problem analysis and solution identification for empowerment in holistic ministry.

One cannot talk of empowerment without talking of literacy. If people cannot read and write, their participation in the development process will be limited at some point. Only one case, the Rushinga cattle project, talked about the literacy levels of people and programs that dealt with literacy.

In some cases, empowerment must occur before significant participation is possible. Some communities are already organized and only need resources. In others, people require assistance to become organized. In some cases people must be helped to learn to help themselves. Often this requires new skill and knowledge, just as in other areas of intervention, such as agriculture or health.

This requires a strategy. We cannot just assume participation by a community or anticipate it as a natural outcome of offering assistance. In many cases, it had to be planned for and facilitated. One of the first aspects of planning an intervention strategy related to facilitating participation is assessing the obstacles.

Obstacles or promoters of participation

According to David Korten and Felipe Alfonso (1985), while policy makers and donors have widely recognized and mandated the need for local participation, the obstacles to actually implementing such participation have received little attention. For participation to occur, suggests Korten, certain obstacles within the implementing agency, within the community itself and often within society must be overcome before participation can adequately occur.

Within the implementing agency, these obstacles include such things as the locus of decision-making (who, how and where decisions are made), the attitudes and values of staff (being learners and not only teachers) and the evaluation systems—who determines what will be evaluated and the stability of personnel involved in the project implementation and management.

Obstacles within the community include the lack of an appropriate local organization to work with or through; the lack of trained leaders; and the lack of organizational skills, poor facilities, factionalism and corruption.

Finally, obstacles within the society can include such things as politics, particular laws and government bureaucracies. Management must recognize that obstacles exist and must be dealt with for participation to have a chance of occurring, and these must be given consideration in project design. Dealing with such issues requires time and money, usually two of the most precious commodities of any project (Korten 1980).

Jean-Claude Garcia-Zamor (1985) also identifies obstacles that must be overcome for the possibility of development participation in planning and management to occur. These include: "(1) the dominance of one group over another; (2) the lack of interest of potential participants; (3) the lack of sufficient time; and (4) restrictions generated by present structures and systems" (p. 8).

Now let us take a closer look at some obstacles to participation.

1. *Person of the implementer.* Our cases reveal that one of the critical components that can be either an obstacle or promoter of participation is the person of the implementer. The experience in the cases (especially the FHI agriculture and AIDS projects, WV Ethiopia's Ansokia program) suggests that participation begins with the attitude of the program implementer and local leaders. Both must believe that the local people have something to contribute. The fundamental underlying assumption is that people have relevant experience and knowledge to contribute to their own development. Despite their poverty or lack of education, people of a given community have learned to survive, if not prosper, in that situation. As people with self-worth and dignity, they have the potential to take charge of their situation.

The cases demonstrate that if the program implementer does not believe that the people are capable of helping themselves, then he or she will see themselves as the one who needs to do everything for these helpless people. The attitude of the program implementer is critical as to whether participation will occur.

If people responsible for the development program do not believe local people have something to contribute, then their behavior will reflect this view. Paternalism and dependency will result. Holism is primarily found in the individual, not in the program.

2. *Community attitude.* The attitude of the local people also has an effect. In Uganda, people had come to feel that the government owed them something, because of their contribution during the war. They felt they should be provided for rather than be expected to provide for themselves.

Also, as demonstrated by the FHI agricultural program in Uganda, a major obstacle can be local leaders who do not believe the people have anything to contribute. The local government representative had stated that he did not believe the local people were capable of managing anything themselves. This became a major obstacle to facilitating participation.

3. *Agency attitude.* Too often the aid agency is eager to help because it benefits their objective in "doing something for" the community or providing a service they have been funded to provide. The agency can then report to its donors the successful use of the resources provided. Any person or community will sit back and let someone else do something for them. What do they have to lose? There is no risk or commitment. This paternalism perpetuates the community's dependency on the agency. This approach is agency-centered, not community-centered.

4. *Culture, respect and relationships.* Understanding the local context, history and culture gives a person the ability to build relationships of trust and respect. These case studies found that identifying the positive and building on the community's strengths contributed to development efforts. Taking time to learn the language and understand local beliefs, customs, traditions and culture provide a basis for effective communication.

We also see that understanding of culture goes beyond ethnic or tribal identity to the history of an area. What development efforts have been tried and failed or succeeded? What is the status of the church? What structure and plans does the government have for the area? Knowing this information was important to the approach taken in these cases. Through an understanding of local culture, building relationships of trust and credibility becomes possible.

This is true not only of expatriates but of national workers as well. Although many of the case implementers are nationals working in their own countries, the area they work in may be different from where they grew up. Learning the language and understanding the culture is just as important for them as it might be for an expatriate coming from a different country.

The local infrastructure and approaches to identifying leaders and making decisions provides a basis for identifying local organizations and individuals to work through. Not being aware of or ignoring the traditional infrastructure of leaders and decision-making can be detrimental to facilitating community participation.

5. *Poverty does not prevent participation.* No matter how poor, every community and individual has something to contribute. The cases demonstrate that identifying and starting with local resources is a key to people's sense of ownership and dignity. Resources such as land, time, ideas, labor and material are often a starting point. Such resources are often overlooked in comparison to what appears to be large amounts of money brought in by the external agency. Too much money applied too quickly can impede local initiative and ownership, as found in the FHI agricultural program. When these local contributions are actually costed (the monetary value of what they would cost if you had to pay for them) and added up, their total value might equal or exceed that of the external cash contributions.

Resources can also include the traditional values of a local society of self-help and extended family, such as the "strong sharing spirit" in the FHI AIDS program and the Rushinga cattle project. Even in the cases of the AIDS programs, it was found that people had something to contribute to the development process. In one case, this involved identifying the community strengths of the extended family and a caring attitude toward those in need. In another, it involved organizing committees to plan and manage the care. The formation of clubs to develop ways to communicate the AIDS prevention message through drama, debates and training was another.

Local institutions, including the church and government offices, also provide a source of resources. Include existing social work and development efforts by the government and other NGOs in the development process.

Methods for facilitating participation

What practical techniques can we employ to facilitate participation? Our cases illustrate two techniques.

The Rushinga cattle project case study said, "[that] the decision to start our work with a feeding program was based on the needs expressed by the community members themselves." Who represented the community and how did they express these needs? Was there a meeting? Who turned up? Were women present and did they speak? Were leaders identified by vote or by consensus? How did people express and then prioritize their needs? These are a few of the questions that we must answer when thinking about facilitating community participation.

In the case of the Rushinga cattle project, the method employed to identify the community's priority concerns is called *participatory rural appraisal* (PRA). This approach involved initial meetings with community leaders to plan the process. Then, a "larger group" was called together to identify and prioritize the community's needs. When is the group large enough to be representative of the community? How does the makeup of the group determine whether or not the poor and marginalized will be heard?

While the case study does not elaborate, PRA also involves identification of local resources as well as needs. The idea behind PRA methodology is to learn from and with the community members to investigate, analyze and evaluate the community's resources and opportunities and whatever constraints on development may exist. Following the analysis of a particular situation, the methodology is also used for feasibility study, identifying, prioritizing and planning project interventions. As a project or intervention is implemented, it provides a means of evaluating progress. Or as a project expands, the PRA method can be used to reassess priorities and resources. This is particularly useful when additional resources have been created through the successes of the past project activities. This also provides opportunities to learn from the project experience. In the Rushinga cattle project, we see PRA being used as a tool to begin the process with the community and then later as a monitoring and evaluation tool.

141

Through PRA, new insights are gained. The community's involvement in determining the lending method for cattle in the Rushinga cattle project clearly demonstrated how local knowledge and experience can improve program outcomes.

The method uses specific techniques for involving the community members in collecting and analyzing information about their community. Some of these techniques include map drawing, wealth ranking, transect (a diagram of main land use zones), seasonal calendar, livelihood analysis and the venn diagram (a diagram that shows key institutions and individuals in a community and their relationships and importance for decision-making).

The WV Ethiopia program refers to its methodology for facilitating participation as the CBTP (community based technical program). According to the case, "[this] approach is designed to enhance participation through facilitation techniques and incorporate program development skills to bring attitudinal and behavioral changes among community members."

A methodology that is not articulated in any of the cases but that is implied in several (FHI AIDS and Chidamoyo AIDS programs) is that of the "appreciative inquiry" approach. This approach involves focusing on the positive—identifying and affirming the good things about a community. Appreciative inquiry asks two questions: 1) What in this particular setting, culture or community makes life possible? and 2) What are the possibilities that provide opportunities for more effective forms of organizing, facilitating and training?

The idea is to build on the best things (people, values, traditions, beliefs) in communities. The assumption is that all cultures and communities have something good in their community. The appreciative inquiry approach attempts to turn the negatives into potentials and the positives into strengths. The process often uses four steps:

1. Discover and value those factors that give life to that community;
2. When the best of what exists has been identified and valued, begin to envision new possibilities;

3. Then engage dialogue, open sharing of discoveries and possibilities, to arrive at an ideal, a shared vision of the community for the future; and

4. Then members of the community find innovative ways to help move themselves closer to the shared vision. They begin the process of constructing the vision.

The references list at the end of this chapter provides a source of practical ideas for facilitating community participation.

Differences observed

What differences appear between the cases and the guidelines for effective development through participation?

Some cases mention community participation or empowerment as an aim, but then do not have a corresponding strategy or intervention to achieve it, as they might have for health or agriculture.

The FHI agricultural program stated that "a study revealed" what the local needs were. The case study further stated that "farmer support was enlisted to begin banana plantation." What would have happened if people had been involved in the process of identifying and analyzing their situation from the beginning? What difference would it have made to their motivation and participation?

As a result of their evaluation, the FHI agricultural program reflected on the importance of working to see what people bring to solve their own problems before bringing in too many external resources. They also found that more time is needed to mobilize the people. The people's genuine involvement would lead to more local ownership and accountability of inputs and resources. The case study evaluation concluded that the focus needed to shift to what people can do for themselves, instead of relying on the agency's handouts.

Although some refer to the importance of participation and sustainability, most of the case material talks about what the agency did for the people or what the leader accomplished. Very little is said about what the people did for themselves.

Bringing help is often a source of power to the giver. This can be perceived as a way to witness for Christ. "Provide," "do for" and "give" are words that dominate some of the project descriptions. While these types of activities can be justified in many situations, they can also be a source of superiority and paternalism by the outsider. Such attitudes, which can be fostered by nationals as well as outsiders, only result in reinforcing the community's dependency. We must avoid using the power that comes with development assistance as the basis for our witness. If we do not, people will be tempted as Simon was to seek the Holy Spirit for power and gain (Acts 8:9-24).

Holistic ministry implications

If a development initiative is following principles of effective development, how does this affect the holistic outcomes? What difference does this make regarding the establishment of new churches or the growth of existing churches?

"Measurable development impacts through the program and discussions the staff conducted with individual community members contributed to the effectiveness of Christian witnessing," wrote the author of one case study. If our good works are not credible from the perspective of the local people, how will our Christian witness be?

Sensitivity to culture, dignity, respect for people, belief in people's potential, affirming people's strengths, reconciliation, accountability, building local capacity, facilitation of local leadership and ownership over decisions and resources are not only approaches to effective development, but also represent biblical concepts and approaches to working with people in community.

Both the Old and New Testaments provide examples of these approaches. Genesis begins with an example of participation. God gives Adam and Eve responsibility over the garden. Nehemiah is the classic Old Testament example of facilitation and participation. From the New Testament, Acts 11:22-30 provides a vivid example of many of these concepts. We find the concept of recognizing, affirming and building on the strengths of the community in verse 23. The importance of the person of the development facilitator is evident in verse 24. In verse 25, we see the need to understand, to

144

effectively communicate cross-culturally and to be a networker and resource linker. The concept of being with the people for an extended time, establishing relationships that enable discipleship and capacity building toward a sustainable movement is seen in verse 26. Finally, we note the concept of taking responsibility for decisions and experiencing genuine partnership through reciprocal sharing of resources in verses 29-30.

Community participation and sustaining "church development"

What do most churches suffer from? They suffer from a lack of resources to build or maintain the church facility or to pay the local pastor. Churches also sometimes lack the ability to sustain the spiritual development of its people.

FHI found in Uganda that pastors could not serve full-time because of the poor income the church provided. If the development interventions are successful and people are both earning more income and growing in their faith, would an expected outcome be increased income for the church? Through small loans that lead to successful businesses and training, Zambuko Trust reports increased personal income, which is being used for church construction and ministry expansion.

What would happen if we apply the same principles of community participation to the establishment and building of the church as we do for the agriculture, health and school projects? How does the idea of building people's capacity to plan and manage their own development relate to the establishment and sustainability of a local church and the believer's spiritual life? If a community can be mobilized to identify and organize resources for building and maintaining a school, why can't the same process work for building and maintaining a church (the physical building or the spiritual one)?

What would happen if we applied these approaches of development facilitation to the task of discipleship, of sustaining the spiritual development of Christians? How can the concepts of community organizing, mobilization, participation and empowerment affect the way we enable Christians to grow in their faith,

145

". . . so that the body of Christ may be built up until we . . . become mature, attaining to the whole measure of the fullness of Christ" (Ephesians 4:12-13)?

Conclusion

Many questions remain unanswered in our quest for effective holistic development. Although our understanding is still incomplete, as revealed in the analysis above, we have learned many lessons. Those who are seeking to achieve effective holistic ministry can apply these lessons elsewhere. Nine proven guidelines for facilitating community participation in holistic ministry have been described. The case study experiences identify five key areas in the development process that can either be an obstacle or a promoter of effective community participation in holistic development.

The analysis also suggests that the principles of participation that were effective in facilitating community development have not yet been fully applied to the task of holistic ministry. It appears that there is more to be gained by applying these principles not only to the "development" activities in holistic ministry, but also to the activities and interventions involved in establishing a sustainable Christian community.

This brief review of the case studies highlights how complex facilitating effective development can be. The challenge faced by those who attempt to work in this area is enormous. Our case study writers are people who are involved in perhaps the most challenging work of our time, a work measured not only by successes, but also by a lack of failures. Clearly, there is significant value in documenting and sharing lessons from holistic ministry experiences.

REFERENCES AND RESOURCES

Bragg, W. 1983."Beyond Development." In *The Church in Response to Human Need*. Tom Sine, ed. Monrovia: MARC Publications.

Bryant, C. and L. G. 1982. White. *Managing Development in the Third World*. Boulder: Westview Press.

———. 1984. *Managing Rural Development with Small Farmer Participation.* West Hartford: Kumarian Press.

Chambers, R. 1985. *Managing Rural Development: Ideas and Experience from East Africa.* West Hartford: Kumarian Press.

———. December 1986. *Normal Professionalism New Paradigms and Development.* Discussion Paper No. 227. Brighton, England: Institute of Development Studies.

———. 1983. *Rural Development: Putting the Last First.* Harlow, Essex: Longman Scientific & Technical.

Cohen, J. M. and N. T. Uphoff. 1980. *Participation's Place in Rural Development: Seeking Clarity through Specificity.* World Development 8 213-235.

Garcia-Zamor, Jean-Claude, ed. 1985. *Public Participation in Development Planning and Management: Cases from Africa and Asia.* Boulder: Westview Press.

Geest, W. V. *The Relationship Between Development and Other Religious Activities and Objectives.* Prepared for the Churches and Development Workshop, June 14-15,1993, Toronto, Canada.

Gow, D. D. and Jerry VanSant. 1983a. *Beyond the Rhetoric of Rural Development Participation: How Can it Be Done?* Washington, D.C.: Development Alternatives, Inc.

———. 1983b. "Participation in community development." *Community Action,* 1(6), 47-51.

———. 1985. "Decentralization and participation: Concepts in need of implementation strategies." In *Implementing Rural Development Projects.* E. R. Morss and D. Gow, eds. Boulder: Westview.

Honadle, George and Jerry VanSant. 1985. *Implementation for Sustainability: Lessons from Integrated Rural Development.* West Hartford: Kumarian Press.

Korten, David C. 1980. "Community organization and rural development: A learning process approach." *Public Administration Review,* 480-511, September-October.

———. 1986a. "Community management and social transformation." In *Community Management.* David C. Korten, ed. West Hartford: Kumarian.

———. 1981. "The management of social transformation." *Public Administration Review,* 41, 609-618.

———. 1984. "Strategic organization for people-centered development." *Public Administration Review,* July/August, 341-352.

————. 1987. "Third generation NGO strategies: A key to people-centered development." *World Development*, 15, 145-159.

————. (1990). *Getting to the Twenty-First Century: Voluntary Action and the Global Agenda*. West Hartford: Kumarian Press.

Korten, David C. and Felipe B. Alfonso, eds. 1985. *Bureaucracy and the Poor: Closing the Gap*. West Hartford: Kumarian Press.

Korten, David C. and R. Klauss, eds. 1984. *People-Centered Development*. West Hartford: Kumarian Press.

Nyerere, Julius. 1976. *The Arusha Declaration: Ten Years After*. Dar-es-Salaam, Tanzania: Government Printer.

Rogers, E. M, ed. 1976. *Communication and Development: Critical Perspectives*. Beverly Hills: Sage Publications.

Rondinelli, Dennis. 1983. *Development Projects as Policy Experiments: An Adaptive Approach to Development Administration*. New York: Methuen.

Tendler, Judith. 1975. *Inside Foreign Aid*. Baltimore: Johns Hopkins University Press.

————. 1982. *Turning Private Voluntary Organizations into Development Agencies: Questions for Evaluation*. Washington, D.C.: U.S. Agency for International Development.

Uphoff, Norman T. 1985. "People's participation in rural development." In *Putting People First: Sociological Variables in Rural Development*. M. M. Cernea, ed. New York: Oxford University Press.

Uphoff, Norman T., J. M. Cohen and A. A. Goldsmith. 1979. *Feasibility and Application of Rural Development Participation: A State of Art Paper*. Ithaca: Cornell University, Rural Development Committee, Center for International Studies.

Voorhies, Samuel J. 1993. "Development Is Participation." *Together*, No. 38, April-June; pp. 14-15.

————. 1992. *From Fund Raising to Implementation: A Case Study of Rural Development Participation in Africa*. Monrovia: World Vision International, February.

————. 1990. "The Ghana rural water project evaluation," p. 27. Monrovia: World Vision International.

————. 1991. "Raising the Chances of Sustainability: Two Attempts." *Together*, No. 31, July-September.

10
A biblical framework
for management practice

Kweku Hutchful

People in communities the world over have, since the days of barter, looked for better ways of meeting their *needs*. A significant development in human history has been the development of *institutions* providing community *services* to meet the needs of people. These institutions mobilize the human, financial and other resources of the community for the production of goods and services in an effective and efficient manner.

The growth of these institutions necessitated the development of a tool to keep institutional behavior in line with its objectives. *Management* became the tool for the efficient running of large, complex institutions and operations. Many principles relating to work efficiency, human behavior at work, managerial functions and roles and organizational development were developed to address challenges in the growing business sectors, and today these form the foundation of management practice in nonbusiness institutions as well.

Most of the management knowledge available to Christian leaders and workers today comes from business-oriented, Western theoretical formulations as well as from institutional traditions; culture; the experience of great managers and so on. In recent years

149

some attempt has been made to relate biblical examples and principles to the task of management.

Biblical foundations

This chapter goes beyond modern management's foundations in the Industrial Revolution and the subsequent development of business management principles. Rather, it explores the roots of management in the creative acts of God as recorded in the opening chapters of Genesis.[1] This chapter develops a foundational biblical framework for management practice by going to the beginning of all things to learn from God the creative Manager. The eternal principles gleaned are then applied to the task of managing *both* evangelism and social action (i.e., holistic ministries) effectively to meet spiritual and material needs in communities.

The account in Genesis of God's creative work is an excellent case study of how to successfully intervene in humanity's chaotic existence and produce very good spiritual and material alternatives for an otherwise hopeless existence. It also provides a significant framework for management practice. God demonstrates good, sound and effective management in the creation of the universe for his workers to emulate. He also is responsible for shaping people into good Christian leaders and workers and positioning them for effective ministries (Jeremiah 1:5; Isaiah 49:1-2, 6; Genesis 45:4-8; Mark 1:17).

Genesis opens with the phrase, "In the beginning God . . ." Recognizing God as the beginning of all Christian ministry has implications for our relationship with him (John 15—abide in him), our behavior (1 John 1:7—walk in the light), our motivation (Matthew 22:37-40—love for God and neighbor) and our resources. God is our resource and, in particular, the source of all the wisdom needed for holistic ministry that results in long-term community security and stability like a house built on the rock (Matthew 7:24-27).

God is more than willing to give us his wisdom for managing. From Proverbs 3:19 we learn that "by *wisdom* the Lord laid the earth's foundations, by *understanding* he set the heavens in place; by his *knowledge* the deeps were divided, and the clouds let drop the dew." It is thrilling to see that Proverbs 24:3 describes the human activity of construction in the same way as the divine work of creation: "By *wisdom* a house is built, and through *understanding* it is established; through *knowledge* its rooms are filled with rare and beautiful treasures."

I would like, therefore, to define this kind of creative management as *the God-given wisdom required for creating order out of chaos and empowering people for good stewardship so that God is glorified and people are blessed.*

What then is this divine wisdom that will enable us to produce abundant, abiding, fruitful holistic ministries and to what extent are they demonstrated in the case studies? The following "Genesis Principles," as I call them, teach us God's way of managing for better results.

Work of creation

"In the beginning God created . . ." (Genesis 1:1). In our first encounter with God we find him busy at work. God began by creating—bringing forth something out of nothing. It is important to acknowledge the fact that in ministry we are coworkers with God in the creation of an abundant life for all people (1 Corinthians 3:5-15; 2 Corinthians 5:18). What we are involved in is the work of bringing into being that which did not exist before, using what God has richly endowed people with. God has richly blessed Africa with rivers, mountains, cultivable lands, forests, solar energy, vegetation, fish, animals and minerals.

The Luke Society (Ghana) reports that, "Ghana is a resource-rich country . . . [and] is the second largest producer of gold in the world." Our ministry should empower so-called poor people to "create" something new out of what God has given. The case studies are full of stories of the creation of new productive activities, new technologies and new capacities for income generation among people who had previously existed only on handouts.

The case study on World Vision Ethiopia's Ansokia program demonstrates the progression from "relief operations to an integrated rural development scheme that is based on multifaceted participatory intervention." From this area, devastated by previous droughts, was created a productive agricultural region self-sufficient in food production with a "dynamic and growing church and Christian community."

This transformation of "a rural community of the hungry and poor . . . [into] a green and fertile area inhabited by industrious farmers" is an example of the work of creation to which we are called —and it is holistic in nature.

We see the holistic ministry of Zambuko Trust resulting in the creation of a "city set on a hill" in Mufakose. From their own income and in partnership with other Christians, the Glad Tidings congregation raised the image of their whole community with their new multipurpose two-story building.

Chaos-vision paradigm

The next three sections below introduce what I refer to as the "chaos-vision paradigm" based on Genesis 1:2. While it is important to start with a clear description and understanding of the chaos confronting communities, it is even more important that there is a crossover from chaos to vision, from a problem focus to a solution focus. Many communities in Africa are stuck in the problem analysis stage, needing help to move on to creative formulations of solutions.

Holistic ministries should demonstrate the processes of creative thinking, envisioning and crossing over from problem to solution, and these ministries should train community leaders to do that for themselves. This will ensure a future and hope for the communities when they are finally left on their own to implement their own solutions to the problems confronting them. The cases demonstrate these processes in various ways.

Chaos

Genesis 1:2 notes that the situation God faced was characterized by emptiness, darkness and formlessness. In seminars conducted around Africa I have often asked participants to describe this situation in their own words. The responses have always included words like confusion, chaos and disorder. Applying these words to

Africa's countries, churches, communities, public institutions, families and personal lives demonstrates how pervasive the mismanagement of the continent is.

Very often, and certainly in the case of the studies we are discussing, the work of creation begins with an appreciation of the chaotic conditions confronting communities. A compelling starting point for holistic ministry is the chaos in human existence.

Management must take the fact of chaos seriously and all the case studies before us identify the multiple faces of chaos in Africa. Among the numerous manifestations of darkness, emptiness and formlessness encountered are:

- ❖ Ethnic conflicts leading to displaced populations; orphans.
- ❖ AIDS and HIV-related diseases resulting in "AIDS orphans"
- ❖ Crime
- ❖ Modernism and the destruction of positive cultural values relating, for instance, to sexuality
- ❖ Poverty
- ❖ Primitive infrastructure (poor educational systems; impassable roads; no electricity, clean water, medical services)
- ❖ Drought
- ❖ Famine
- ❖ Disease
- ❖ Slums; congested and underdeveloped areas of poorly built dwellings
- ❖ Witchcraft

Creative thinking

What do we do about all of this chaos confronting poor communities in Africa? The "brooding" activity of the Spirit of God in Genesis 1:2 demonstrates the way forward. Modelled for us here is the activity of careful reflection. We must take time to reflect on a community's problems until the problems become the source of inspiration and the light begins to dawn as our imaginations paint a new future characterized by order, peace and plenty.

To make time to "brood" and think creatively along with the community is the key to a fruitful holistic ministry. Much as disasters and situations of poverty often require speedy responses, we must always precede such action with creative thinking or we will create greater levels of dependency by our unimaginative interventions, resulting in short term gains at the expense of security and stability in the long run.

Holistic ministry needs to go beyond mere assistance to a group of people in need. It is partnership with God in bringing a "new universe" into being in communities all over the world. It requires creativity characterized by vision that is translated into specific, measurable goals and results.

The Ansokia I ADP case study demonstrates the place of creativity and innovation in holistic ministry, patterned after the wisdom of God who is the Creator, who makes all things new and who is continuously doing new things. The case study reports a growing capacity of the community leadership for "adopting innovations" as well as a growing general community interest in various innovations and improvements.

Innovation is a key management concept deriving from God's creative involvement with his universe. Holistic ministry should be characterized by creative thinking and should empower community leaders to similarly engage in the kind of creative thinking that leads to new initiatives. The case reports that "community members are now more aware of their problems and their environment. They are in a position to take initiatives . . . to implement integrated development programs."

Vision

It is this creative thinking that releases visions of new communities. God gives visions to his partners in holistic ministry. The examples of Joseph and Daniel are particularly instructive (Daniel 2:20-23, 45; Genesis 41:39-40). It is clear from most of the case studies that the interventions in communities are guided by clear visions of what the future states of those communities could be.

The case study on the AIDS Awareness Project (Uganda) recounts of the project's beginnings: ". . . an expatriate and a Ugandan pastor sat down to pray and ask God what he would have them do about the destruction caused by AIDS." The Luke Society case study reports that "[John Oduro Boateng] had a growing vision to help the poor among [his] own people in Ghana through health care and evangelism."

Without vision, people perish. This is true of both the community leaders and the intervening agency. The case study on Food for the Hungry's agricultural project (Uganda) notes that "most people are so busy dealing with today's problems that they have little time, energy or ability to plan for future needs." Holistic ministry should address this need for envisioning among community leaders in practical ways and through modelling.

Vision comes from several sources: it may come from God through prayer and the study of his Word; it may be the result of looking at what others are doing; or it may emerge from a study of the challenges and needs in the community. Whatever the source, one person usually captures the vision for change, and that person then has the task of motivating and mobilizing the whole community behind that vision. Where the visionary is an outsider the task of building community ownership becomes an even more important strategic undertaking.

Order creation

Beyond creative thinking and envisioning lies the task of making things happen. Again the answer lies in the story of the Creation. God created order out of chaos. Management, like worship, thrives on order. God is a God of peace (order), therefore those who worship him must do so not only in spirit and truth, but also in an orderly fashion (1 Corinthians 14:33, 40). Good management is, in fact, an act of worship. We need to let our ordered lives confess the lordship of Christ in our midst.

In Genesis 1:7, 9, 11 we see God bringing about order through the separation and the gathering of water and other elements and the classification of plants and trees, according to their various kinds. God used the organizational processes of separating, gathering and classifying to create a new physical environment that became the home of the human race.

One of management's main tasks is to confront chaos and confusion wherever it is found, pushing back the boundaries of disorder to create a new order through effective organization. Restorating order to our national, institutional, community, family and personal affairs is a number one priority.

All the available evidence points to a need to significantly strengthen organizational skills for creating order in African rural and urban communities. Ethnic conflicts, political activities and mismanagement have wreaked havoc with whatever disciplined community life existed in rural communities. In all their activities, holistic ministries must model, teach and demonstrate strong organizational skills and systems for the creation of order.

The case studies show us several examples of order creation activities:

- ❖ Income generating activities
- ❖ Employment creation
- ❖ AIDS education
- ❖ Counselling
- ❖ Home-based care for AIDS patients
- ❖ Health delivery
- ❖ Commodities programs
- ❖ Agricultural programs
- ❖ Provision of water
- ❖ Evangelism and church planting
- ❖ Leadership development
- ❖ Advocacy

These activities form the heart of holistic ministry activities. It is, however, important not to see them as just project activities but as order creation activities that progressively uproot the culture of chaos and confusion that is so rampant in Africa and introduce better community organization.

Another dimension of this organizational phase is the development of community organizations or institutions to carry on these order creation activities in a sustainable manner. Many of the case studies refer to existing organizations in the communities, some of which are well organized and could be used as the focal point of successful awareness creation and mobilization efforts.

In other cases, the intervening agency had to put in place structures and systems to carry out its order creation activities. The Chidamoyo Christian Hospital created a home care team as an integrated part of the hospital care of AIDS patients. At a later stage volunteers were recruited from local churches to work with and supplement the work of the home care team.

Managerial culture for transformation

Other key management principles relating to the holistic ministry that emerge from our study of the Genesis Creation story include productivity, quality, evaluation, results-orientedness, communication and spiritual warfare. These principles together form a *managerial culture* within which people can pursue successful community transformation. The case studies demonstrate each of these.

Productivity

First, the principle of productivity. Genesis 1:20, 22, 24 relate the fact that God thinks and acts in terms of abundance and productivity: "Let the water teem with living creatures . . . be fruitful and increase in number . . . let the land produce living creatures . . ." It is clear that the focus of holistic ministry is not to continue giving handouts but to bring the community to the point where it is productive and can sustain itself through abundant supplies.

The Ansokia I ADP is an excellent example of this. The project reports an increase in total area under cultivation from 7,980 hectares to 8,218 hectares and the development of vegetable production from zero to "a significant contributor to diet and is a cash crop in 15 peasant associations." Providing improved tools, seeds and techniques led to an increase in yield per hectare of 50 percent. Surplus production brings in more cash to fill gaps in financial needs.

Productivity is also experienced spiritually in the increasing numbers of disciples, trained leaders and churches. John Oduro Boateng and his staff of the Luke Society (Ghana) have planted 24

157

new churches in the last five years. Its holistic approach is demonstrated by the growth in health facilities as well—"community health centers in 22 remote communities."

Quality

Not many of the case studies refer to the quality of their activities in communities. Genesis 1:31 indicates that God had a concern for qualitative work—he saw all that he had made "and it was very good."

Holistic ministry that is properly managed according to God's standards should share God's concern for quality intervention. The Luke Society reports that "the Kasei Clinic has a reputation for quality care," and notes that the clinic has "an almost 0 percent infection rate on hernia surgeries and very few patients have hernias that recur." This quality health care attracts wealthy clients whose fees contribute to the financing of the project.

The maintenance of quality service at all times is important for both agencies and communities. Again, holistic ministry should demonstrate both quantity (productivity) and quality to the communities as essential dimensions of creative management, patterned after God's divine example.

Evaluation

It is clear from the Genesis account that God evaluated continuously during and at the end of the Creation. Seven times in the first chapter of Genesis we are told that God saw what he had created and it was good—meaning that what had come into being conformed to the standard that God had in mind before speaking them into being.

Most of the case studies provide us with evaluations that focus on obstacles facing the ministry and improvements required for greater effectiveness and efficiency. The evaluation of the United Baptist Church's ministry in Rushinga not only led to better practices but also the decision to teach Bible college students and pastors the need to "minister to the whole person and meet physical, spiritual, social and economic needs."

158

Result orientedness

The work of creation calls for a strong result-oriented attitude and goal setting. In Genesis 2:1-2 we read that the heavens and earth were *completed*, and God *finished* the work of creation.

Many lack this strong sense of finish in Christian ministry. The seemingly never ending task of developing new communities (in both material and spiritual senses) should not result in a lack of goal setting. Rather, it is critical that we establish finishing points at which we can evaluate and determine new directions.

God's key leaders in the Bible were noted for finishing God's assignments—Moses finished the tabernacle; Nehemiah finished the wall; Paul finished his ministry to the Gentiles; Joseph and Daniel finished long, productive government careers; Jesus said, "It is finished."

It is an indication of good management that all the case studies clearly identify key results arising from their involvement in the various communities. It is extremely important that we express visions and dreams in terms of key result areas with goals for each area at the beginning of the work of creation. Project proposals should clearly indicate expected results so that it would be clear to the community and the agency that they have crossed various finishing lines.

Holistic ministry should of course incorporate both spiritual and material results. The cases amply demonstrate both: increased food production; better infrastructure; loving health care; spiritually transformed lives; churches planted; income generated from new businesses; trained church and community leadership; and behavioral and cultural changes. In addition to the spiritual and material dimensions, results should also reflect long- versus short-term interests; quality versus quantity; and visible versus invisible outcomes.

Communication

The divine model of the work of creation illustrates the power of life-changing communication. God created the universe by the power of the spoken word. Several times we read the phrase "God said" and note the powerful effects of God's words.

At the human level, effective communication is essential for the motivation and mobilization of support and involvement. Nehemiah's testimony and challenge to the unproductive, discouraged, disinterested Israelites led to the response, "Let us rise up and build" (Nehemiah 2:18 RSV). Truly the tongue, though little, can set on fire—in positive, as well as negative, ways. Today, effective communication in management involves not only the face to face spoken word, or the written word, but also the several forms of electronic media and the information super highway.

Holistic ministry practitioners find themselves often moving between communication on the Internet with international partners and communication by signs and through interpreters in rural settings where mode of dress and facial expressions facilitate or hinder effective communication. In Christian ministry we go beyond the forms and tools of management communication to the power of the Spirit to help us penetrate the deep, inner hearts of men and women through our communication. This important process of consultation and communication with the local community, church and government leaders to motivate and mobilize does not receive adequate treatment in the cases.

Also important is the place of effective communication in order-creation activities—such as the use of relevant media in awareness creation and community education. The AIDS awareness project (Uganda) notes as a critical ministry assumption the fact that "culturally adapted communications will result in a greater knowledge of God's Word and a better understanding of how to deal with AIDS, and music and drama are effective forms to communicate in this culture." The description of the project's development process includes the training of church leaders in the presentation of the "Challenge of AIDS" to their own parishes, as well as the preparation of music and drama to support the AIDS awareness information.

In Genesis 11:6 God underlines the importance of unity and agreement for breakthroughs: "If as one people speaking the same language they have begun to do this, then nothing they plan to do will be impossible for them." Effective management communication creates understanding and provides direction for the whole group.

Spiritual warfare

The Luke Society (Ghana) case study says that idolatry and demonic bondage are "factors prohibiting prosperity and well-being within the country." Affirming the reality and power of evil spirits, Society staff members attribute their successful holistic ministry to "prayer, fasting, good planning and participation."

Obviously, many involved in holistic ministry in Africa fail to see spiritual warfare as an effective management strategy. Genesis 3 focuses our thoughts on the confusing, destructive and deadly activities of Satan. The holistic ministry practitioner in Africa works in an environment characterized by satanic activity and is subject to satanic influence and attack. Our analysis of threats in the environment should incorporate this supernatural dimension, calling for "prayer 'without ceasing' for the program and beneficiaries [and] listening to that 'still, small voice' [of God]" (a key principle of the AIDS awareness project, Uganda).

The people dimension

The next set of principles explore the people and team aspects of holistic ministry and community transformation. These principles examine such issues as effective ways of working with people, promoting stewardship, building collaborative relationships and teams and providing quality leadership.

Working with people and stewardship

Genesis 1:26-2:17 introduces the concept of stewardship and God's relationship with humans as coworkers. One key management lesson emerging from this passage is the need to acknowledge the dignity of a human being as someone created in the image of God. This calls for respect for people. This principle of *respect* is important for holistic ministry practitioners, given the fact that a ministry's target groups are often described as "the poorest of the poor," "unable to help themselves" and "feeling hopeless and worthless." These phrases that development organi-

161

zations use to describe communities can themselves contribute to the loss of dignity.

The goal of holistic ministry should be to be coworkers with God in restoring dignity and dominion, returning to communities the control of the circumstances in which they live, bringing them into abundant living and helping them become a self-respecting and respectable community.

Another key lesson is the need to give people *responsibility*. God gave Adam the responsibility "to work [the garden] and take care of it" (Genesis 2:15). God also entrusted Adam with the task of naming the animals (Genesis 2:19-20).

Restoration of respect involves the acceptance of meaningful responsibility. In all of the case studies, we see community and church members accepting the responsibility of transforming their communities and caring for the weak and young.

The Zambuko Trust case study notes that "the large number of unemployed people in the cities is having very distressing consequences." This affects both national and church development. Zambuko's loan and training ministry helps people like Terezia Mbasera to exercise proper stewardship of resources, to create jobs and employment and to support Christian work through their local congregation.

Holistic ministries must demonstrate the kind of trust in people that makes them responsible workers rather than beggars. We must accompany this with the necessary training as well as checks and controls to ensure that the trust is not refused or abused (Genesis 2:16-17). Train and trust—the keys to the effective creation of responsibility.

A final lesson relates to the principle of *provision*. God made adequate provision for Adam's stay in the garden (Genesis 1:29-30; 2:8-18). A key aspect of holistic ministry is the provision of the necessary information, tools, funds and personnel to enable the community to begin to address its problems and opportunities. It is important to address the issue of expectations early in the project so that no misunderstandings are created as to what will or will not be provided. The cases, of course, revolve around the many kinds of spiritual and material services provided to assist with meeting the needs of communities.

Partnerships

The cases report successful efforts at building good relationships and creating cooperative efforts with community and church leadership and with government and donor agencies. This is an important dimension of effective creative management. The exciting stories of project management in the Bible all point to the need for strong relationship-building skills for cooperative efforts. Nehemiah provided a good example of this in the way he gained governmental, religious and community support for the construction of the wall (Nehemiah 1-3).

The Genesis 2 account of Adam and Eve provides some basic principles of teambuilding. Starting, in verse 18, with the acknowledgement that one individual (or agency) cannot do it alone, the story establishes the need for human help. Important factors that facilitate effective teambuilding include complementarity (2:18, 23); loyalty and commitment (v. 24); unity (v. 24b); and transparency and respect (v. 25).

The AIDS Awareness project (Uganda) identifies a key role of the project manager as that of "coordinat[ing] with church leaders and key people to secure cooperation." This interpersonal role of leaders leads to informational and decisional roles so vital for effective management.

In many cases, specialist agencies are brought in—especially in the area of evangelism—to assist the agency and local churches in fulfilling their goals. For example, Life Ministry teamed up with the agricultural project of Food For the Hungry (Uganda) and local churches to present the Jesus Film.

Leadership

The cases do not indicate in much detail how these key principles of managing people and teambuilding apply to staff issues within the development organizations themselves. It has been the experience in Africa that competencies for effective management of people and projects have not always been in abundant supply. In some situations, the "poorest of the poor" are the leaders of development organizations who exhibit inadequate leadership, management competencies and maturity.

Complaints about lack of respect, poor work organization, unclear levels of authority, unrealistic expectations, inadequate provision of equipment or funding, insufficient housing and lack of team spirit are common in organizations involved in holistic ministries. The high levels of staff commitment are not always matched by adequate personnel and human resource development policies and proper staff care. Given the potentially stressful conditions under which staff work, it does not help to have inefficient administrative and managerial leadership.

Leadership development at organizational and community levels is critical for sustainable holistic ministry in Africa. At the organizational level, this includes the intentional development of nationals for both middle and top level management positions. Focus leadership development efforts on the people who have already demonstrated a commitment to the agency's vision, values and ethos and who are capable of incarnating this in the community. At the community level this would involve the careful equipping of recognized and emerging local leadership for more effective leadership practice.

Resource mobilization

The provision of adequate funding for projects emerges as an issue of major concern in some of the cases. Beyond the general issue of maintaining adequate funding, there is the more critical issue of finding funds for both dimensions of the ministry to achieve both material and spiritual goals. Even more challenging is the issue of financing evangelistic and church planting activities when funds are from secular sources and designated for only relief or development activities.

Another major challenge facing practitioners of holistic ministry is donor disinterest in the spiritual aspects of development work. Sometimes there is pressure to abandon spiritual activities and there are threats of withdrawal of funds. What is the way out?

The Luke Society (Ghana) case demonstrates the need for disclosure of the ministry's Christian identity as well as the creation of multiple sources of funding to match the needs of both dimensions of holistic ministry. A variety of sources support the Luke Society's activities, including:

- ❖ The government
- ❖ Luke Society International headquarters (ministry partner)
- ❖ Project income (hospital fees on a sliding scale)
- ❖ International agencies, such as WHO (donations in kind)
- ❖ Local sources such as local government authorities, traditional authorities and direct beneficiaries
- ❖ The business community
- ❖ "Ministry business ventures"—income generation activities (hiring of equipment, farms, cooperatives)
- ❖ Loans for seed capital

Some of the funds were earmarked for the clinic only, others for evangelism and church planting only and still others were for both. The funds and donations in kind are generated from local, national and international sources. The Luke Society staff approach the private, public, non-governmental organization (NGO) and church-related sectors.

Given the diversified nature of its funding and the strong commitment to holistic ministry that pays equal attention to both material and spiritual matters, the Luke Society project can choose which funding agencies to work with. As a policy, it only works with those whose interests match closely the identified needs of the community and have no objections to the sharing of the gospel.

What then is the key? Boateng calls it "collaborative links—[a] willingness to work with other ministries, government, and non-government organizations and local leaders to achieve common goals." To achieve this and to continue increasing the number of linkages requires planning, prioritization and hard work. It is important for practitioners of holistic ministry to see donor cultivation as a key result area of the ministry that requires goalsetting and action plans.

But resource mobilization also calls for prayer and dependence on God. Boateng sees his network of donor relationships as a gift from God. Quoting Nehemiah, he attributes his success to "the good hand of my God upon [us]" (Nehemiah 2:8 KJV).

What the Luke Society has done is to put into practice, in the area of resource mobilization, the biblical principle for managing growth. Moses (Exodus 18 and Numbers 11), the disciples (Acts 6:1-7) and the fishermen in Luke 5:1-11—they all brought in more people to spread the increasing burden created by God-given growth. Similarly, to avoid the neglect of the material and spiritual dimensions of holistic ministry, agencies should make efforts to cultivate a wider network of donor relationships with different organizations at the local, national and international levels. In the great resource mobilization story of Exodus 35-40, Moses mobilized 603,550 men to give to the building of the tabernacle. No wonder they had "more than enough" and had to stop the people from giving more (Exodus 36:4-7). We need to throw the nets wide, trusting God for those who are willing and whose hearts move them to support effective holistic ministry.

Conclusion

Poor communities have both material and spiritual needs. Characterized by several manifestations of chaos, these communities need agencies focusing on holistic ministry to help with the creation of order and the meeting of their needs.

Beyond this, they also need these agencies to model leadership and management values, principles and practices for sustainable community development and government. The Ansokia I ADP case pinpoints the need for more training and "promotion of the managerial capacity of community members."

This calls for an exhibition of eternal and enduring principles of leadership and management that are applicable in all cultures. God models such management in the creation of the universe. Our holistic ministries must pattern their management on God's model if they are to become cities set on the hill and lights on lampstands to the communities they work in. Then their light will shine before these communities, that these communities may see their good deeds and give glory to the Father in heaven—not to the gods of secular management and technology.

NOTES

1   This chapter is based on the author's forthcoming book on creative management, which is based on Genesis 1-11. These thoughts were originally developed by the author in 1988 as introductory material in management training seminars for Christian leaders in Africa.

11
Sociological and anthropological reflections

Olivia N. Muchena

It is important to recognize the diversity of people on the African continent. Africans are not a homogenous mass from Cape to Cairo, but differ in culture, language and colonial experience, to mention a few indicators. The cases presented in this book—coming from Ghana, Ethiopia, Uganda, Mozambique and Zimbabwe—demonstrate some of the diversity that can be found among African cultures.

There are enough similarities, however, to allow the designation of African culture. The case studies also demonstrate some of these similarities. Common threads running through the cases include:

❖ A holistic versus a compartmentalized view of life;
❖ Cultural attributes that facilitate or hinder the development process;
❖ Similar attitudes to and experiences of the role of money in development; and
❖ The use of indigenous knowledge, structures and relationships in bringing about development.

My reflections will seek to draw out these themes as they have been raised in the cases.

Holistic ministry in a compartmentalized reality

The typical African of the past (if there is such a person) looked at life as an integrated whole. The spiritual and the material, the religious and the secular, the political, economic and social were all linked, intertwined and sometimes made one continuum. The traditional African view of land illustrates this point. Land belonged to God (and therefore could not be owned by any person); it was administered by political cum spiritual leaders—the chiefs; land was held in trust on behalf of the living, the dead and those yet to come. Land management included scientific (e.g., terracing) and metaphysical (taboos related to land and agricultural practice) aspects. Agriculture was a way of life, a business and a profession.

What has happened to this holistic perspective of life? Z. Sardar (1988) refers to Goontilakes use of the metaphor of knowledge hills to describe the historical and current status of indigenous knowledge systems. Hills of knowledge reflecting different civilizations (China, India, Europe, Africa) existed before the dominance of modern scientific knowledge. In more recent times, the scientific system has levelled all the other hills. But, according to Sardar, ". . . this is not a world hill; it is only a regional hill masquerading as a universal phenomenon" (1988:13).

This Western world view, which the African has imbibed through education, colonization and other processes, is very much compartmentalized. There is a strict separation of the sacred and secular, politics and religion, private and public, economics and social life. Christianity, in the way it came to our continent, promoted this type of compartmentalized thinking. It usually presented itself to us through the mission station, an island surrounded by the unconverted heathen.

Modern educated Africans have embraced this compartmentalized world view. This is evident in the economic and scientific determinism that characterize our development thinking and planning. Unlike the Southeast Asian countries, we have not maintained the traditional with the modern in terms of providing positive African values to undergird the development process. One wise old man I interviewed in the Manicaland Province of Zimbabwe put it this way: *"Chirungu chakauya, hapana chichayera* (Nothing is sacred anymore, since the coming of the white man)."

The challenge of holistic ministry is how to live, do and experience our faith in the development arena. It is how to return the sacred to its rightful place at the center of everyday existence. The primary way this was done in many of the cases was through the living examples of the people who carry out holistic ministry. Those who demonstrated holistic living were able to communicate these values to those with whom they worked. Some examples:

- ❖ "One method used to introduce people to Christ was . . . personal sharing with people during visits to their homes and gardens by FHI staff" (Food for the Hungry International, Uganda agriculture program).
- ❖ "The exemplary life of the staff attracted many people from the community to come to Jesus" (World Vision Ethiopia, Ansokia I ADP).
- ❖ "People have given their lives to Christ . . . as a direct result of . . . staff involved in a wide range of [Christian witness] activities . . . carried out during non-work hours" (World Vision Mozambique).

The power of this sort of holistic example can be seen in the way that some of the people who participate in the programs became holistic ministers themselves. In the Zambuko case, Terezia Mbasera witnessed to her employees and provided accommodation for them. At the Chidamoyo Hospital, Ephraim and Juliet learned they had AIDS and also learned to put their faith in Christ. They then started a church in their home village, which now has 100 regular worshippers. In Uganda the family members of AIDS victims who receive training through Food for the Hungry's program began reaching out to other families in similar positions.

Effective holistic ministry in a holistic culture must go beyond the personal example of the staff. The program itself must address development holistically. World Vision's program in Ansokia, Ethiopia, involved a multidisciplinary technical team, evangelists, community leaders, government officials and many others. Food for the Hungry's AIDS Challenge program in Uganda works through local churches, addressing the spiritual, social and physical aspects of AIDS prevention.

On the other hand, some of the cases seemed to illustrate a more compartmentalized Western way of thinking about development. World Vision in Mozambique appeared to keep its church relations project separate from its other activities. Other cases seemed to avoid relationships with local political structures, as if there was no role for politics in the development of a community.

In the context of a traditional African culture that saw life holistically, there must be congruence between the spoken witness of the organizations carrying out holistic ministry, the design of their programs and the lifestyle of their staff. The organization—whether NGO or church—and its staff must be able to "walk the talk." Holistic ministry that compartmentalizes life is a contradiction in terms.

Facilitators and obstacles to development in African culture

In every society certain aspects of the culture facilitate development, while others retard development. The cases show how this is true in African society. In almost all the cases the family and community are presented as key institutions in the development process. Closely related to these are the African values of sharing, mutual obligation, inclusivity, involvement, collaboration and self-reliance. These values provide strong bases for promoting development, while ignoring them often leads to obstacles or hindrances to development.

Family: The heart of African culture is the extended family system and the intricate network of kinship relations and obligations. This is a much different paradigm from the Western concept of a nuclear family. Many cases showed how this extended family network could be used to promote development. The Chidamoyo Hospital saw how AIDS affected the whole family and included family members of people with AIDS in its counselling sessions.

Community: In many ways the community is a further extension of family relationships. It has its own well-defined leadership structures, systems of responsibility and obligation and codes of conduct. Development efforts have a better chance of success if they can fit within these structures and systems. Some of the cases had no problem working within the community because their leaders and staff came from the communities they served. These included the Luke Society in Ghana and Zambuko Trust in Zimbabwe. In other cases the leaders learned about the community by becoming a part of it.

Beyond understanding community values and mores, the development project should seek to build the capacity within the community to care for its own needs. This comes through clearly in the World Vision Ethiopia case where the committee chairman said, "The money is ours, the work is ours, the responsibility is ours."

Sharing and mutual obligation: The reciprocal obligations of the African extended family provided a way for sharing resources and meeting needs while still respecting the value of each person. For example, a girl receives support and instruction from her aunt while she grows up and then, when she is older, is expected to provide the same sort of assistance to her niece. (This close-knit sharing is a firmly embedded part of African culture, and exists regardless of a person's economic status. This sharing mentality is not caused by poverty, as the two Uganda cases suggested.)

Development efforts should build on this cultural value. They should not only help people to help themselves, they should help people to help others. By doing this they affirm the value of the people they work with, allowing these people to play their appropriate roles and fulfill their obligations within the community. The United Baptist Church does this in Rushinga by having farmers repay their "loan" of a cow by passing their first heifer on to the next family in line. In Uganda, the farmers in the Food for the Hungry project share their produce with their church and neighbors. They also provide banana shoots to other farmers to help them start gardens.

Involvement and inclusivity: The Shona have a proverb which says, "*Ane benzi ndeanerake, rika tamba anopururudza.*" It means that the insane person is part of the social life of the community and

173

others still need to appreciate his or her human dignity. Within the community there is to be no deliberate seclusion, isolation or alienation of the less fortunate. The worst thing that can happen to an African is to be closed out or ostracized. The two AIDS cases show how education and counselling for members of the family and the community can help ensure that those with AIDS can maintain their place in their society.

Collaboration: The African is a consultative being. Africans in precolonial societies (and in some current rural societies) decided the affairs of the community through discussions and debate until they reached a consensus or majority view. The channels for participation varied depending on factors of age, role in society, gender and the particular issue involved. People expressed their views through debates, discussions, poetry, music, dance and drama.

This sort of decision-making by palaver can be extremely frustrating to outsiders, especially those with a Western view of time. But it is the process by which a community can decide and move forward together. In Ghana, John Oduro Boateng shows the importance of collaboration by meeting with the chiefs of each village to get their approval for working in their area. In Ethiopia, the World Vision staff in Ansokia developed their plans through discussions with government officials and community leaders.

Self-reliance: In most African societies human beings have certain character traits that distinguish them from other species or even other races. Certain behaviors or activities are considered to be dehumanizing. A typical African child was brought up to believe that constant begging and borrowing was dehumanizing (in Shona, *zvinobvisa unhu*). The values of hard work and self-reliance were instilled and internalized on the basis of this *unhu/ubuntu* concept.

Many of the cases emphasize the need to maintain and build the dignity of the people involved in holistic ministry programs. The Luke Society in Ghana talks about the need to develop businesses to provide a way for people to earn their own income. In the Rushinga cattle project and in the Food for the Hungry agricultural project farmers have to repay the assistance they have received by sharing their production with others. Zambuko Trust treats its clients as enterprising business people who not only repay the loans they receive, but also pay interest that sustains the Zambuko organization.

Cultural traditions and institutions can also hinder the development of communities and societies. The cases highlight two obstacles to development that come from within African culture—the spiritual heritage of traditional African societies and the traditional division of labor between genders.

Spiritual heritage: As described above, the traditional holistic view of life held by Africans did not make distinctions between the physical and the spiritual. Africans have long maintained contact with the spirit world through the spirit medium and the *n'anga* (traditional healer or witch doctor). In African traditional beliefs, the spirits of the dead are still active in this world. Illness and other misfortune can be the result of curses placed by other people and carried out by the spirits of ancestors. This is a deeply ingrained part of African culture. Educated and urbanized Africans will still consult *n'angas* to cure a sickness or improve their fortunes, even as they see medical doctors and go to church.

Some of the cases (the Luke Society, World Vision Mozambique) mention the strong spiritual opposition that they have encountered in their work. They have had to cast out spirits from people who resisted their work. To the Western ear this idea of exorcism as a key to development may seem strange, but those who work in Africa understand why the casting out of demons played such a critical role in the ministry of Jesus while he was on earth. The belief that suffering and bad luck come from spells and ancestral spirits can induce a fatalism that stymies any attempts at development. The casting out of spirits demonstrates that the power of God is greater than the power of the ancestral spirits. If people can also learn that this powerful God loves and cares for them, they can begin to believe that their lives can be better.

Gender roles: Most traditional African societies are dominated by the males. In Shona society, women's access to the use of land came through husbands or other male relatives, yet the fields are known as *munda waami Chipo* (the field of Chipo's mother). This was because women did most of the work in the fields. In other activities involving hard labor women carry most of the burden, such as caring for AIDS patients and orphans or getting involved in community development activities. Few of the cases presented discussed the role of women in the community or the division of labor by gender in the development programs.

God and mammon

Almost all of the case writers talk about money, either because they need more of it or because money has affected the way they do their work. Yet we must also look at money from a spiritual and cultural perspective. The Zambuko case calls money "the most material of all commodities." Money, however, also has a spiritual side. Jesus called it the spirit of mammon and said that it was impossible to serve both the spirit of mammon and the Spirit of God (Matthew 6:24). In Africa these words of Jesus carry deep meaning. A look at the history of money on this continent may show us why.

In Northern and Western Africa units of currency have been used for centuries to facilitate trade between the tribes of Africa and those of Europe and the Orient. One of the commodities traded for money (and guns and liquor) was human lives through the slave trade. In the agricultural societies of Southern Africa, barter and sharing were the primary means of exchanging goods. Money was forcibly introduced when the colonial powers needed workers for their farms and mines. The governments introduced poll taxes that could only be paid with money. This forced African men to work in the mines or on a white man's farm to earn the money needed to pay the tax. The result is that money, while essential to life in most parts of Africa today, still has an alien and alienating feel to it.

The development work reviewed in the cases involves money and sometimes, as in the case of World Vision Mozambique, staggering amounts of money. In all of these cases the development work requires funds and other resources generated outside a community being brought to bear on problems and needs within a community. While the money may address the need, it can also have severe unintended consequences.

As I wrote earlier, African children used to be taught that begging would cause them to lose their humanity. Today we see children and adults begging on almost every major city street. In doing this, they are only emulating their governments, which beg for loans and donations from other nations. I have often wondered what culture shock our ancestors would get if they were to wake up and find begging and borrowing institutionalized on a continental scale!

Well-intentioned development programs and their use of money can take some of the blame for this change in the culture. Where once the community felt responsibility to care for the needs of people in the community, now they look to relief and development organizations to care for those needs. Where once communities sought to improve their lot through their own work and resources, now they think that the only way to develop is to get money from someone else. Why do the work yourself when there are development agencies with more money than you will ever see in a lifetime looking for places to give it away?

Not only have African individuals, communities and countries become dependent on donations, so have Christian development organizations. Most of the cases involve the use of government funds to carry out some portion of the holistic ministry programs. While most of the writers say this funding does not prevent them from carrying out holistic ministry, it is bound to have some impact on the way they implement that ministry. John Boateng says that he will not accept funds from donors that do not want him to preach the gospel. He also says that the major obstacle to their income generation program is the lack of seed capital.

Jesus was right. Money has a corrupting spiritual force. While development programs need it to do their work, they must be careful that they do not end up serving money instead of God. When the money is being used to carry out holistic ministry, it is sometimes hard to tell the difference.

Using indigenous knowledge systems

Throughout this reflection I have sought to use the knowledge and understanding of African culture to explain holistic ministry as it is portrayed in the cases. This is sometimes called an emic-etic approach. The emic-etic perspective is used to explain how insiders and outsiders view a given phenomenon from different cultures or world views. W. H. Goodenough (1981: 16) explains it this way:

> When we describe any socially meaningful behavioral system, the description is an emic one to the extent that it is based on elements that are components of that system, and the description is an etic one to the extent that it is based on conceptual elements that are not components of that system.

Rattan (1988) indicates how in development literature cultural endowments (the emic perspective) are often viewed as obstacles to technical or institutional change. One reason for this view is that cultural endowments are analyzed from an etic perspective using predetermined general concepts that come from outside the culture being studied. A large component of the emic perspective is comprised of religion, taboos, myths and related ethnic ideologies and values. These elements of indigenous cultural systems appear irrational from an etic perspective. M. Howes (1985) summarizes the perceptions or the essence of indigenous knowledge systems in current literature as mystical-irrational, utilitarian or intrinsic. Reaction to indigenous knowledge by researchers, educators, development professionals and institutions depends on the perceptions they hold. Table 11.1 on page 179 illustrates these perceptions, responses and the potential contribution of indigenous knowledge.

The point of all this regarding the subject at hand is this: For ministry to be truly holistic, it must be seen as holistic by the person receiving the ministry and not just by the person providing it. For the person providing the ministry to know whether it will be holistic in its context, he or she must be able to see the ministry from within the knowledge system of the people being served. This is as true for urban Africans going to work in rural areas as it is for people from other continents coming to work here.

Gaining this knowledge requires a different way of relating to the local community, for they must become partners in the ministry, helping to educate the "ministers" to the realities from their perspective. One Zimbabwean agricultural extension worker put it this way, "The most important thing is to know people's traditions and humble yourself before them. Don't try to be different or act as a 'professional' from the outside" (M. Sofo et. al., 1980:30).

To be able to carry out effective holistic ministry, we must understand the way the people we work with perceive us and our work. This requires allowing ourselves to be taught by the people we too often call "beneficiaries." We should do this not just because it makes it easier for us to implement our development projects. We should do this because it helps us to learn and grow and become better people as the result of the ministry our "beneficiaries" provide to us.

Conclusion

I have been using Shona proverbs and sayings throughout this reflection, so I would like to conclude with just one more. It goes

Level of Perception	Response Evoked	Potential Contribution
Mystical-Irrational	• Obstacle to development • Inferiority complex, embarassment • Dismiss, ignore • Useless	Beliefs, myths as encodement of knowledge
Utilitarian	• Acknowledge and partially accept validity • Romanticism, idolization • Scepticism	Substitute, compliment, hybridize Western knowledge system
Intrinsic	• Curiosity • Desire to learn more, i.e., research and development	Joint ventures, dialogue, participation; analysis for generation of knowledge and values

Table 11.1. Responses to indigenous knowledge systems:
Levels of perceptions, responses and potential contribution
(adapted from M. Howes [1985] and indigenous knowledge systems literature).

like this: "*Njere moto unogokwa* (Knowledge is like live coals)." This saying refers to a cooking fire in a rural village. In the Shona tradition, no one owns a fire. To start a fire you would go to a neighbor who had a fire going, take some burning coals and use them to start your fire. A while later another neighbor may come and take some of your coals to get her fire started.

I see the holistic consultation in the same way. The cases all tell us of places where the fire of God's Spirit is moving. Each of the case writers will bring with them live coals of knowledge from those fires. When we bring them all together in this book we will have a very nice bonfire going. But I pray that it will not stop there. I pray that we will all take live coals from this fire away with us, and that we will spread them around in our own countries and the places we travel to. I pray that the result of this consultation will be many more fires throughout Africa, many more examples of Christians ministering holistically, demonstrating God's love and sharing the fullness of life to which he calls all of us.

REFERENCES

Goodenough, W. H. 1981. *Culture, Language and Society*. London: The Benjamin/Cummings.

Howes, M. 1985. "The uses of indigenous technical knowledge in development." In *Indigenous Knowledge Systems and Development*. D. Brokensha, D. M. Warren and O. Werner, eds. Lanham: University Press of America, pp. 335-352.

Muchena, O. 1990. *An Analysis of Indigenous Knowledge Systems: Implications for Agricultural Extension Education with Particular Reference to Natural Resource Management in Zimbabwe*. Ames, Iowa: Iowa State University.

Sardar, Z., ed. 1988. *The Revenge of Athena: Science, Exploration and the Third World*. New York: Mansell Publishing Limited.

Sofo, M., D. Topouzis, S. Horst, S. Amakaje, N. Karrichi, S. Owaltara, C. L. Morra, and L. Kilimviko. 1980. "Making extension work for the African Farmer: The key to Africa's future." *African Farmer*, 4, 28-33.

12
Theological reflections

Kwame Bediako

Behind every instance of authentic Christian ministry there lie divine impulses, and it is not the easiest of tasks to capture such impulses in all their intricacies in human words. My theological reflections are an attempt to respond to the case studies by drawing attention to some matters of theological interest. Though not all those issues were raised by the authors themselves, nevertheless they seemed to me to arise from the nature of the ministries described, and in a number of instances by the perspectives of the practitioners themselves. The case studies raise a number of questions with wider theological implications for how we are to understand our Christian calling in the world.

Image: Biblical and Christian or Western and secular?

All the case studies rightly take their contexts seriously, and in a number of them there is an especially acute awareness of the peculiar convergence of socioeconomic, cultural and even spiritual realities which appear to conspire to make up the particular African context in which the Christian intervention is taking place. In some of the case studies, there is the sense that the ministry is engaged in "spiritual warfare," doing battle with cultural and religious world views and patterns of thought that are felt to be inimical to the intended Christian goal. In one instance, the prevalence of witchcraft as a sociocultural habit of mind in the context is identified as a major obstacle.

The larger theological issue raised by such consideration is the question of what underlying image of Africa and African life is shaping and determining the Christian response and the earnest attempts at seeking Christian solutions. How far is that image derived from a theological viewpoint, or is it in fact deeply influenced by secular thinking?

The question is important because of the prevailing mood in secular Western thought of what is sometimes referred to as "Afro-pessimism," namely a sense of the intractability of many of the continent's socioeconomic and political difficulties. It is only a short step from this diagnosis to seeing the problems as somehow peculiarly African. In the light of scenarios of Africa such as that presented by Robert Kaplan in his article "The Coming Anarchy" in the *Atlantic Monthly* (February 1994), where do Christians committed to holistic ministry in Africa derive their image of the context they seek to serve?

Ministries that have to deal with AIDS and its associated problems are, to my mind, among the most vulnerable to the onslaught of this "Afro-pessimism" so prevalent in Western analyses of the African condition. There is a real danger that AIDS itself becomes somehow an African problem, rather than the *human* problem that it is. Whereas many Western nations have the means to mask and somewhat marginalize the AIDS scenarios in their contexts, most African nations lack these means and devices. Thus, African "promiscuity" comes to the forefront, while Western homosexuality falls into the background of attention. The net result is that Africa appears more blameworthy. The point is that Christian intervention through holistic ministry in Africa must be kept from being pushed into the situation where it fails to recognize how utterly human, not to say "normal," Africa's particular problems are. Africa's problems are not new in world history, and it is a delusion of Western secular thinking to imagine that the Western world is raised above the kinds of scenarios that are the focus of attention in Africa.

What I am arguing for is not a naive or triumphalist view that glosses over problems in context, but a biblical and Christian viewpoint that sees these problems as opportunities for men and women of faith, with the help of the God who is always working (John 5:17) to seek biblical solutions. What is being argued for here is a prophetic vision like that of the pre-exilic and exilic prophets of the Old Testament, who were able to interpret current realities and point the way to the future that God was preparing for his people.

It was the same prophetic insight which inspired Augustine—faced with the collapse of the Western Roman Empire in the fifth century A.D. and the resulting widespread pessimism and despair—to refuse to believe that the fall of Rome was the end of the world. From my sense of the case studies, it is my conviction that practitioners of holistic ministry in Africa need this prophetic insight as Christian theological armor against the negative currents of modern secular assessments of Africa. A truly biblical and Christian understanding of the world, history and human existence will mean looking for the positive realities in the African context and at the same time maintaining a more critical distance from Western analyses.

It becomes possible, from such a perspective, to see that the remarkable Christian expansion on the continent in the twentieth century and the continent's current problems converge to make Africa a privileged arena for Christian engagement. Africa's present status as one of the heartlands of the Christian faith worldwide, therefore, make it a key context for discovering and shaping new forms and patterns of Christian mission and ministry.[1]

Gospel and culture

A number of the case studies speak of cultural and religious world view changes, of the transformation of lifestyles with coming to faith in Jesus Christ, and coming to Christ as Lord as a crucial element in the objectives they are seeking to achieve. While I affirm the importance of these objectives, my concern is whether the practitioners go far enough. The larger question is, what do the practitioners of holistic ministry themselves understand by the gospel, and what is the character of the transformation that the gospel is to bring about?

In the light of the recent history of ethnic conflict and strife involving large numbers of persons presumed to be Christians, it still remains to be explained why such problems appear to have been untouched by a Christian impact. It may be too easy an explanation to suggest that the people involved were not "born again." Rather we may need to raise fresh questions regarding the adequacy of the understanding of the nature and task of the gospel, not only on the part of those who are evangelized, but also on the part of those who engage in Christian witness and ministry.

In many of the case studies, the goal of the evangelism that takes place within the holistic ministry is shaped by an understanding of the gospel that focuses on the number of believers, rather than on the depth of Christianity's sociocultural and religious impact. My unease is that there are dimensions of the evangelistic mandate that we appear to continually miss in our efforts to carry out the Great Commission.

The Great Commission in Matthew 28 is not about numbers or statistics, important as these are. The Great Commission is not about the percentages of national populations that we may consider to have been "reached" or remain "unreached" with the gospel, important as these considerations are. Our Lord did not say, "Go make disciples of some people or even of a large percentage of the people of the nations." What he commanded was, "Go make disciples of the nations, go make the nations my disciples."

The Great Commission, therefore, is about the discipline of the nations, the conversion of the things that make people into nations—the shared and common processes of thinking; attitudes; world views; perspectives; languages; and the cultural, social and economic habits of thought, behavior and practice. These things and the lives of the people in whom such things find expression— all of this is meant to be within the call of discipleship. Nationality itself is brought within the purview of discipleship.

True evangelization and conversion is turning over to Christ all that he finds when he meets us, and asking that Christ cleanse, purify and sanctify us and all that we are, eliminating what he considers incompatible with him. This means, for example, that in our discipline of the nations God calls the peoples of the earth to bring under the lordship of Jesus Christ all those things in their lives that they reckon sets themselves apart from others, and which they sometimes use to distinguish themselves from others as though superior to them. We cannot regard a nation or people as adequately encountered by the gospel, even if they constitute a large Christian population, when their cultural habits of thought, behavior and practice show that those features are being kept independent of the lordship of Jesus Christ.

From this perspective, it becomes evident that our calling to communicate and live by the gospel is more difficult than we usually assume it is. It calls for resources far beyond what we allow for in our normal institutional and perhaps even personal priorities as Christians and Christian organizations and churches. It requires commitment and levels of sacrifice—in time, study, energy, serious prayer, deep and long-term engagement with people and various practices and habits of mind and behavior, applying the mind of Christ to a whole range of social, political, religious and cultural realities—at levels which few of us, probably, are willing to make. In other words, we may not assume that we are working with an adequate grasp of the gospel.

Biblical models for holistic Christian ministry in Africa

Each of the case studies has rightly emphasized the importance of the Christian lifestyle of the practitioners themselves. Nowhere is ministry reduced to simply the execution of programs or projects. There is also in some studies a specific recognition of the power of the incarnational model in which the Christian worker is with the people in their problems, bearing their problems with them and walking with them in seeking God's will in solving their problems.

What seems to me to be much less clear is the extent to which the practitioners discern the full ramifications of the incarnational model in Christian ministry. Do the practitioners perceive their role as agents of change purely in the narrow sense of bringing relief

185

from distress and a new sense of the love of God in the gospel, or do they see themselves as witnesses to the coming of the kingdom of God to a people, which in turn will reshape that people's sense of their past, their self-understanding and their vision of the future?

The apostle Paul is the supreme example here in his commitment to the Gentiles as expressed in Romans 15:16 (RSV), where he describes himself as:

> *A minister of Christ Jesus to the Gentiles in the priestly service of the gospel of God, so that the offering of the Gentiles* [that is, the things that have to do with the Gentiles] *may be acceptable, sanctified by the Holy Spirit.*

I believe this text has much to say about how Christians committed to holistic ministry may understand themselves and their role. In the context of Paul's discussion (Romans 15), he had earlier (v. 8) spoken of Christ as "a servant of the Jews on behalf of God's truth, to confirm the promises made to the patriarchs" and therefore bringing to fulfillment the aspirations of the Jews. Christ's achievement then opens the way for the grafting of the Gentiles into the new people of God (v. 9). In a bold stroke, Paul draws a parallel between Christ's achievement for the Jews and his own achievement for the Gentiles, seeing both in the sweep of God's activity in universal salvation history.

The point, then, is that Christians involved in holistic ministry in today's world need, with appropriate humility, to discern their role in a similar vein—not as purveyors of a commodity, whether spiritual or physical, but as facilitators of a people's own discovery of their heritage as the children of Abraham and grafted into the one universal community of God's people in history. In the vision of Revelation 7:9-12, where a great multitude from every nation, tribe, people and language are found praising God in their diverse linguistic and cultural expressions, we see that the task of the gospel is not the salvation of our "souls" apart from the cultural embodiment of our lives. Rather, the purpose and goal of the gospel is the redemption of cultures and the cleansing of all cultural forms of life and expression so that they come to express praise and adoration of the one Living God and our Lord Jesus Christ. If this is the consummation of the gospel's task in the world, what new insight does this biblical vision bring to our conception of holistic ministry?

Holistic ministry and the church

A good number of the case studies give evidence of positive relationships with existing churches in their area. In a few cases the effectiveness of holistic ministry has resulted in the spiritual renewal of existing churches. This is important and needs to be seen as more than a practical convenience or a strategy for effectiveness. Since in biblical perspective the church is the primary agent of God's activity in the world, and holistic ministry is not simply a purveyor of spiritual or physical commodities, the relationship between programs in holistic ministry and the church are of fundamental theological importance and need to be well thought through.

Where holistic ministries are the initiative of parachurch organizations, relationships with existing churches are not always easy, and there may be the temptation to take the easy way out and operate in total independence from them. Working toward a relationship of mutual spiritual accountability with local churches, however, is part of what it means to be holistic in taking both the gospel and the context seriously.

If the relationship with the local church is seen to be important in this way, a further question arises as to relationships with donor agencies, in particular where the donor agencies are secular. Some of the case studies seem to indicate that their ministries are to a considerable extent driven by the project priorities as set by their donor agencies; others seem to have a clear idea of their basis for cooperation, so that where secular agencies are unwilling to accept their Christian and evangelistic thrust, they are prepared to refuse funding from those sources. It is a matter of theological integrity for Christian agencies to ask themselves how far they can go in concealing their religious convictions regarding social questions in initial contacts with secular funding agencies. Perhaps the fundamental question being raised for us here is the matter of the spirituality of money itself, and how such an appreciation affects our Christian intervention, as well as the integrity of the church as an instrument of God's action in the world.

The meaning of "holistic"

This remains perhaps the most elusive of all the issues raised in the case studies. "Holistic" is obviously a key word for the purposes of this consultation. Reading through the publication that grew out of the Asia consultation held in Chiang Mai, Thailand, in November 1994, I get the distinct impression that in Asia too, as in Africa, there is confusion about the nature of holistic ministry. This, I am sure, is not for want of trying. Rather, as Bryant Myers comments in one of his chapters in *Serving with the Poor in Asia: Cases in Holistic Ministry* (T. Yamamori et al, eds. Monrovia: MARC, 1995, p. 190),

> There is still a long way to go to conceptualize and find expression for a thoroughly seamless spiritual-physical understanding of holistic ministry.

Our problem may well lie there. We, as evangelical Christians, are acutely aware of the distinction between the spiritual and the physical; at the same time, we are also eager to affirm their inseparability in our Christian call to service. We are instinctively conscious of an implicit hierarchy of values in our Lord's words: "What good is it for a man to gain the whole world, yet forfeit his soul [life]" (Mark 8:36)? And yet, in our observation of his actual practice, we are gripped by his consistent ministry to the whole person—spiritual, physical, emotional, social and economic—and by what appears to be his refusal to make the kind of distinctions with which we struggle. Being "holistic" may therefore have to do more with ourselves, first and foremost, and much less with the programs and projects that we execute in the interest of "holistic ministry."

At this point, I wish to raise a number of questions for our consideration. Does holistic have to mean a whole wide range of different activities? Does it have to imply comprehensiveness in terms of programs? Does being holistic have to involve a balancing act between "spiritual" and "material" priorities?

And therefore does the attempt that one finds in some of the case studies to fit the ministry into this rigid grid of comprehensiveness in the end lead to a loss of focus? Here I use focus not in the sense of strategic planning, but in the more fundamental sense of theology.

In other words, what is the nature and task of the gospel that makes ministry holistic? Is it not the point of the parable of the Good Samaritan that we may also define holism as addressing the "one thing . . . needful" (Luke 10:41-42 RSV) in specific circumstances? What is extraordinary is that while in the parable of the Good Samaritan it is the Samaritan's response in concrete, "material" action that is commended, in the text mentioned above it is not Martha's busy activity in serving the Lord, but Mary's "inactivity" in sitting down and listening to the Lord, that is commended. It is, perhaps, equally remarkable that the two accounts follow one another in Luke's account (Luke 10:25-37 and Luke 10:38-42).

Is it the nature of the project, or is it the quality of Christian response and intervention, that makes a ministry holistic? Just as the gospel is a Person, not a program, so holistic ministry has to be personal, not programmatic.

This also means that questions relating to the quality of the discipleship of the Christian who is committed to holistic ministry are an integral part of what we may understand by holistic. Another way of expressing this thought is to say that the messenger is part of the message. In Paul's understanding in 1 Corinthians 15:1-11, the work of the grace of God in his own life was part of his testimony to the power and credibility of the gospel.

Perhaps there is no more challenging way of conceiving of the dynamics of our service of the gospel than in Paul's insight that part of every genuinely pure motivation in Christian service is also the Christian worker's own sense of need for the same gospel that he or she seeks to incarnate and to impart to others. For Paul, an essential component in his understanding of his earnest and heroic attempt to communicate the gospel was also his sense that he too needed to receive, in ever increasing measure, the same gospel. If he was so keen to "become all things to all men so that by all possible means I might save some" (1 Corinthians 9:22), it was also because of what he said next: "I do all this for the sake of the gospel, that I may share in its blessings" (v. 23). In the words of Roland Allen, "In revealing [Christ] to others, we reveal him to ourselves" (*Missionary Principles*, Grand Rapids: Eerdmans, 1964, p. 98).

Some points of significance

The practitioners of the various ministries are to be commended for the range and degree of Christian response to human need that their ministries signify. It is important to recognize that a Christian response to the various situations of human need represented is itself of a theological nature, in that it presupposes a theological, or perhaps more simply, a biblical-religious reading and interpretation of the particular situation or context that is being addressed. In other words, a theological perspective is not just the fruit of theoretical reflection on any particular set of actions. A theological viewpoint also underpins those very actions.

In the well-known parable of Luke 10, the Samaritan's response to the man in need was just as much a theological one as was the response of the priest and the Levite. Jesus' way of dealing with the initial highly theoretical question posed by the teacher of the law—"What must I do to inherit eternal life?" (v. 25)—shows that a theological response can be just as down-to-earth as are the realities of our human existence.

Yet there seems to be more significance to the various ministries described than may appear initially. That significance is, above all else, intellectual. The success of these Christian interventions constitutes an effective counterpoint to the kind of prevalent pessimistic assessments made and repeated about Africa. The Food for the Hungry International AIDS work in Uganda demonstrates the deep impact that a sustained modeling and teaching of a Christian life can have within a community; the Chidamoyo Christian Hospital work in Zimbabwe provides an illuminating instance of Christian influence in community building; and the Food for the Hungry agricultural project in Uganda introduced a major new departure for the community. Perhaps most interestingly of all, Zambuko Trust in Zimbabwe demonstrates how, under the impact of the gospel, money can become de-mystified and be understood as a resource under God, to be used responsibly—a deep and unique Christian insight.

All these—to mention only a few—point to the fact that in African life, the Christian faith appears to function as a historical category, capable of providing a key for self-understanding and collective consciousness, as well as a community's sense of their future. This constitutes a major intellectual breakthrough and is all the more important in view of the fact that in the late twentieth century the African continent has become, perhaps surprisingly, one of the heartlands of the Christian faith.

Some critical questions

Nevertheless, some critical questions remain.

1. In AIDS awareness programs, is there any connection made between African "promiscuity" and Western homosexuality? How aware are AIDS patients in Africa of the alleged connection between the virus and United States germ warfare experiments? Or is AIDS simply presented as an "African" problem? In other words, how far is holistic ministry also about imparting, through the holistic gospel, a holistic perspective on local problems?

2. It may well be that African societies need to be challenged from the perspective of the ascetic ideal in Christian teaching and history. For a continent that initiated and perfected monasticism in the deserts of Egypt and Nubia, how is it that African tradition is now so massively committed to marriage, to the extent that an adult spinster or bachelor is almost an abnormality? Might the view taken of Christian service in African societies be significantly affected by a more widespread appreciation of the single state?

3. A final observation on the meaning of "holistic" may also be in order. In view of the general evangelical tendency to stress

the primacy of word over deed, a biblical passage such as John 5:31-40 (TEV) may bear some meditation. Verse 36 is particularly apposite:

But I have a witness on my behalf even greater than the witness that John gave: the works that I do, the works my Father gave me to do, these speak on my behalf and show that the Father has sent me.

Might there not be implied in this teaching by our Lord the thought that the nature of Christian truth is not that of assertion, but rather that of recognition? If this is granted, then may we not say that Christian holistic ministry is about creating the opportunity, through the mutual interpenetration of word and deeds, for others to come to a similar recognition of who Jesus is for them, as for us?

Conclusion

Our discussion of the dimensions of holistic ministry will continue for a long time, as will our efforts to achieve holism in ministry itself. In this quest, it may well be that it is not many things we seek, but the one thing needful. We would all agree that that one thing is Christ.

But so long as we have not yet reached the full potential of our "knowledge of the Son of God and become mature, attaining to the whole measure of the fullness of Christ," as Paul expresses the thought in Ephesians 4:13, so long will our learning continue.

NOTES

1 For a further discussion of what "image" of Africa emerges from an appreciation of its *Christian* significance, see the chapter, "The place of Africa in a changing world—the Christian factor" in my book, *Christianity in Africa: The Renewal of a Non-Western Religion*. Edinburgh: EUP and New York: Orbis Books, 1995, pp. 252-267.

13
Missiological reflections

Roy Musasiwa

In reflecting from a missiological perspective upon the case studies before us our first task is to understand what mission is. Ever since the beginning of the missionary movement initiated by William Carey in 1792 the understanding of what mission is has suffered in four ways.

What is mission?

First, the term "mission" became narrowly defined as evangelism taking place in other geographical places and cultures. Any social concern such as the building of schools and hospitals was seen as merely an aid to evangelism, as bait to attract people to Christ. Biblical reflection will not bear such a truncated view of mission, which limits the concept geographically (something that happens in other countries or cultures) or conceptually (only if it is evangelism and church planting). We can be thankful that all our case studies implicitly, and sometimes explicitly, reject this view of mission.

The second misconception of mission came as a reaction by the ccumenical wing of the church to a privatized view of mission as evangelism. This emphasized mission as social concern with hardly any concern for the eternal lostness of human beings without Christ. Hungry stomachs must be fed. Ignorant minds (in terms of the three Rs: Reading, 'Riting and 'Rithmetic) must be informed. Oppressed people must be liberated. Evangelism was subtly mocked as advocating "pie in the sky by and by." What is refreshing about the ministries represented by our cases is that although they have been prompted by the need to respond to various social problems (what missiologists have described as the "Cultural Mandate"), they all recognize that the "evangelistic mandate" must be an intrinsic part of that process. Among the critical assumptions helpfully brought out by both of the Food For the Hungry projects in Uganda, but also implied by the other projects, is that a commitment to Jesus Christ as Lord changes lifestyles, and that such a change of lifestyle is necessary in the fight against poverty or AIDS.

A holistic definition of mission as consisting of both the evangelistic and the cultural mandate opened the way to the third problem: that of defining mission as everything the church does. The late David Bosch in his *Witness to the World* complained that such a usage of "mission" was inflationary, and then joined Stephen Neill in stating that if everything the church does is mission, then nothing is mission. John Stott's definition of mission as "everything God has sent the church to do in the world" goes some way in helping us to understand the holistic view of mission without thereby making the definition so all-embracing as to make it lose its impact. John Stott proceeds to state that "everything God has sent the church to do in the world" can be summed up by two generic terms—evangelism and social concern.

The problem arising from Stott's understanding of mission as evangelism plus social concern is that these two concepts continue to compete for supremacy. But in a situation of human suffering and alienation, deciding the priority of evangelism versus social concern can be largely an academic exercise. Moreover, this can only be a matter of interpretation, for the Bible nowhere categorically emphasizes one over the other. Paul Hiebert's systems approach to humanity, which sees a dynamic interaction of the spiritual, social, cultural, biological, physical and psychological dimensions of life, would save us from this debate over the hegemony of these concepts.

The fourth problem is an understanding of mission that is too anthropocentric (what humans do), or ecclesiocentric (what the church does), rather than theocentric (what God does). Too much development, even by Christian organizations, fails to distinguish itself from secular models of development. Part of the reason for this is that such models of development do not demonstrate that they derive from the triune missionary God.

So what definition of mission could satisfy all the above concerns: the concern for theocentricism, for the missionary nature of the church and the holistic nature of the task of mission? After a fruitless search for such a definition in the available missiological literature, I have had to coin my own definition, which will undergird my comments on the projects before us. Mission is God's activity through the church for the establishment of his kingdom and the total salvation of humanity. This gives rise to four major considerations when we analyze the cases of holistic development before us:

- ❖ The theocentricity of mission
- ❖ The world of humanity as the primary object of God's mission
- ❖ The church as the primary agent of God's mission
- ❖ A methodology of mission that is incarnational, contextual, empowering and sustainable.

The theocentricity of mission

The concept of *missio Dei* (God's Mission) arose within missiology out of the recognition that mission only makes sense because our God, eternally existent as Father, Son and Holy Spirit, is a missionary God. The church is in mission only because God is in mission. And God is in mission to establish his kingdom—his divine rule—and to effect his concern for the total salvation of humanity.

The whole missionary enterprise originates from the love of God the Father. Ever since Adam and Eve sinned and so alienated themselves from God, we see God reaching down and calling, "Adam, where are you?" The coming of Jesus was the ultimate expression of the love of God. "For God so loved the world that he gave his one and only son . . ." (John 3:16).

There are two important implications concerning God as the source of mission. First we have to ask about the extent to which the projects originate out of a sense of a call from God. It is unfortunate that most development projects are donor-driven, arising because donors who have their own agendas have come into a community and offered to do something about the needs they have identified in the community. The community acquiesces to such development, not wishing to "look a gift horse in the mouth." Unfortunately, such donor-driven development sometimes comes with a great price. The Food for the Hungry AIDS project, Zambuko Trust and World Vision Mozambique all point out constraints imposed by secular donors either in forbidding their funds to be used for religious purposes or in insisting on a distribution of condoms as the answer to the AIDS problem. The danger of allowing secular donors to play the major role in funding projects (such as 87 percent for World Vision Mozambique) is that the projects then seem to owe their existence to donors than to God, and therefore are more accountable to the donors than to God. This is what the Luke Society has successfully fought against by refusing any donor money that interferes with their evangelistic mandate.

The mere existence of a need—whether for food, health or employment—does not by itself constitute a call for initiating a project. But a conviction that God is sending the church to meet these needs in the name of Christ is essential if such a project is to be truly Christian. This is where prayer and the Word of God play a crucial role in the genesis and execution of Christian development programs. Most of the projects under review make it clear that they originated from the Christians' understanding of the teaching of Scripture. The element of conviction born out of prayer, however, has not been made explicit in most of the projects, although it probably played a big role. One strong exception is the Food for the Hungry AIDS program, which states, "The project began when an expatriate and a Ugandan pastor sat down to pray and ask God what he would have them do about the destruction caused by AIDS." This is a heathy acknowledgement that mission is indeed *missio Dei*.

The second implication of mission originating from the loving heart of God lies in the motivation of love that must characterize such development. Our cases are replete with illustrations of this principle. The Chidamoyo (Zimbabwe) AIDS program has a biblical justification for its existence as carrying God's love to AIDS victims and their families through consoling, reconciling, loving and ministering. It was that same love that motivated Dr. Boateng of the Luke Society to live under rough conditions to reach the Ejura district in Ghana for Christ.

If God the Father is the source of mission, then God the Son is the exemplification, par excellence, of that mission in practice. The kingdom promised in the Old Testament was inaugurated at the first coming of Jesus, who revealed God's intentions for the world: forgiveness of sins (Luke 7:48-50); conquest of evil, suffering and death (Matthew 12:28; Luke 4:18-21; Matthew 11:5) and the bringing of a new order of things which overturns common assumptions about power and the value of people (Luke 6:20ff; 13:30). Yet even though the kingdom of God has been inaugurated, it still awaits its consummation, a final day when God's intentions revealed in Jesus will be triumphantly fulfilled.

The Holy Spirit is God's power and the executor of God's mission through the church. The disciples were told to wait for power from on high before commencing the mission before them. "But you will receive power," said Jesus Christ, "when the Holy Spirit comes on you; and you will be my witnesses in Jerusalem, and in all Judea and Samaria, and to the ends of the earth" (Acts 1:8).

Why is there a need for power? Because in a sense mission is about power encounter. Jesus came to establish the kingdom of God in a world dominated by Satan, the prince or ruler of this world. Each person who comes to know Jesus and to be liberated from Satanic bondage is a blow to Satan's kingdom. It would of course be in Satan's interest to resist the expansion of the kingdom of God. This is why we must engage Satan in spiritual warfare so that the kingdom of God, which has already been initiated by the coming of Christ, can be expanded: "Thy kingdom come." For this reason the Luke Society reports on traditional practices that promote idolatry and demonic bondage, preventing the prosperity and well-being of the community. Witches, wizards and fetish priests hold great power over the people. The response of the Luke Society is fasting, prayer and deliverance. Similarly the Rushinga project talks of burning the charms of converts and an exorcism after an all-night battle in prayer. These and other cases demonstrate the indispensability of the Holy Spirit to our mission.

Humanity as the primary object of God's mission

God's mission is directed primarily to the anthropological and not to the cosmic world. It is directed to humanity as historical beings and not as an abstraction. It is also directed to humanity in its total context, which includes the physical, spiritual and social aspects. This is not to ignore the cosmological world, for human beings are stewards of the environment that God has entrusted to us. Therefore a project like World Vision's Ansokia program is quite right to include environmental concerns as one of its thrusts.

Yet God's primary missionary concern, as exemplified by Jesus, is toward the human race, created in God's image, yet corrupted by sin. This sin, as noted by C. René Padilla (1985) and other missiologists, is not just a private spiritual affair between an individual and God. It is also social (separating one person from another) and is manifested both in individuals and the very structures of society.

Into this tragic situation of humanity the mission of God brings the gospel of salvation. Salvation is constantly talked about in two dimensions. First, it involves deliverance from the power and the consequences of sin, enabling people to return to God and to their neighbors. Second, as Padilla (1985) says, "It is transference to the messianic kingdom which, in anticipation of the end, has been made present in Christ." David Bosch (1991) points out that in Luke the verb "save," from which we derive the noun "salvation," includes the healing of the sick. Indeed for Luke salvation has five dimensions: economic, social, physical, psychological and spiritual.

Therefore Padilla warns about avoiding two extreme concepts of "salvation." One extreme sees salvation as only applicable to the "soul," the benefits of which are mainly in futuristic terms, the present only being a preparation for the hereafter. This attitude easily leads to a withdrawal from the world and its problems and the setting up of Christian ghettos. The other extreme sees salvation only in the limits of this present age and is expressed only in terms of economics, society and politics.

When taken together the projects, as already noted, are concerned with all the dimensions of the human race (spiritual, social, physical, psychological) and of the society in which humanity lives (economic, social, political, legal and ideological). It is this aspect of the projects that brings out the comprehensiveness of the kingdom of God that must continually grow until it is consummated in the creation of the new heaven and earth at the second coming of our Lord.

The projects demonstrate this concern for the world of humanity by reporting on:

- ❖ Transformed relationships with the Lord (all the projects report on people becoming Christians).
- ❖ Transformed horizontal relationships: Christians becoming members of evangelical churches, as happened in the Ansokia program).
- ❖ Value change, as in the two Food for the Hungry projects.
- ❖ Economic empowerment as reported by most of the projects.

Unfortunately there is little evidence in the projects of addressing the structural evils of society. The tendency is just to relieve the symptoms of pain caused by that evil instead of addressing the evil itself.

The church as the primary agent of God's mission

The church, in simple terms, is the worldwide body of Christ consisting of all those who have trusted Jesus as their Savior and acknowledged him as their Lord. This understanding of the church universal has always needed a concretized expression. Hence the Bible more frequently talks of "church" in terms of local churches. Although denominations are not specifically mentioned in the Bible, they are an extension of the local church concept. Local churches that bind themselves to each other by reason of sharing common doctrinal emphases, and for the purpose of facilitating what each local church cannot accomplish on its own, become identified as a denomination. Then God raised up parachurch (from the Greek para, meaning alongside) organizations to work alongside the churches to accomplish tasks that churches could not easily do because of denominational differences or lack of expertise.

Because the church is so closely related to the triune God of mission, it must necessarily be God's primary agent for mission. Of course God is sovereign, which means he can choose to use secular institutions just as he used Babylonian and Persian kings to accomplish his purposes in the Old Testament. Yet these are more in the nature of exceptions than the rule. The primary agent for mission remains the church.

Let us now consider two missiological implications.

1. The need for holistic ministries to be closely related to the work of the church in its concretized expression.

It follows from the description of the church given above that parachurch organizations must facilitate the work of churches and in some ways be accountable to them for what they do. Projects that are directly owned and run by churches or denominations (Rushinga cattle, Chidamoyo AIDS) have experienced no conceptual problems in this respect.

The other projects that run as parachurch ministries have struggled with this issue with varying degrees of success. The Zambuko Trust case has clearly articulated the struggle involved here. The writers have made insightful comments on the negative effect of aid bypassing the local church and being channeled directly to the community on the one hand, or being channeled through the local church on the other hand. The writers then claim that Zambuko has found a solution to this dilemma consisting of equipping individuals in the local churches through employment creation. These individuals then empower their churches. This is said to be an effective way to "build the capacity of the local church to carry out holistic ministry, to enable the church to reach out with the love of Christ to all who suffer in its midst." The work of Glad Tidings in Mufakose is then given as a shining example of such capacity building. The problem of Zambuko is that there is no indication of any account-ability or formal partnership structure to the church or churches that claimed to be empowered by Zambuko. And because Christian borrowers enjoy no special attention over non-Christian borrowers (the only qualification is the ability to repay the loans), it is difficult to credit Zambuko with having found the answer to the dilemma that they have articulated so well.

Other projects show a similar struggle in defining their link to the church. The Luke Society actually plants churches and this is highly commendable. It is not clear, however, what its relationship is with these churches. The impression gained is that this is a para-church organization that at times behaves like a church.

Perhaps the best model is one of parachurch ministries working *with* and not just *for* or without churches. This is a model of part-nership. The Food for the Hungry AIDS project in Uganda sees the church as the primary implementer of the program (e.g., through music and drama), with Food for the Hungry serving as a facilita-tor and trainer. The World Vision Ansokia program also gives a high place to the idea of working with the church as a means of changing the people's value system. Hence World Vision facilitated the planting of an evangelical church there. As the writer puts it: "The experience of Ansokia I ADP shows that the existence of a dynamic and growing church and Christian community is an indis-pensable factor for sustainable transformational development." Similarly World Vision Mozambique started a church relations pro-gram that aims at strengthening the work of churches and para-church organizations in that country.

2. The church as both the medium and the message

The second implication of our discussion of the role of the church in mission is the fact of the church being both the medium and the message.

The church is the medium in the sense of being the primary agent for communicating the love of God and the message of salva-tion. Most of the projects under review show the positive impact of the church being the medium of God's message of salvation. The United Baptist Church has been very effective in the Rushinga area. In 1984, 250 baptisms took place, leading to the planting of a church and later the planting of other churches in the surrounding areas. In the Rushinga area alone, there are now seven churches that all began from the original food distribution. Some of the Christians from the original church are already in full-time ministry. This clearly shows the effectiveness of a church being the medium of both the cultural and the evangelistic mandate.

We need to bear in mind, however, that the role of the church goes beyond being the medium to also being the message itself. In other words, the church must embrace within itself the very values it is preaching, if that preaching is going to have any impact. This is why the delivery of ministry "packaged in love," as noted earlier, is so valuable. It agrees with the Lausanne covenant, which declares: "We affirm that we who proclaim the gospel must exemplify it in a life of holiness and love; otherwise our testimony loses its credibility." Another relevant affirmation from Lausanne states: "We affirm the urgent need for churches, mission agencies and other Christian organizations to cooperate in evangelism and social action, repudiating competition and avoiding duplication." The Luke Society demonstrates this principle at work. They talk of "building supportive relationships" and "building collaborative relationships" as one of the key principles they follow, as long as this does not compromise the Christian witness of the society. By repudiating competition and avoiding duplication the Society makes its message credible, and has in fact become the message itself.

There are only a few disturbing methods of ministry that seem to be inconsistent with the values that the church must hold. For example, why should the United Baptist Church-sponsored Marombe-Burai cooperative go into tobacco growing, when it is known that this product is responsible for destroying so many lives? Does the need for cash outweigh the ethics involved? The Zambuko case also raises the question of the ethic of lending money at the bank rate of interest, or close to the bank rate, obviously resulting in some people struggling under the debt burden. It is known that bank interest rates are set with a *profit* motive, whereas a Christian group should lend with a *love* motive. Zambuko has explained the loan policy by referring to the high cost of servicing small loans, the need for Zambuko to offer training to the borrowers and the need to eventually become self-sustaining without continually depending on assistance from outside. These explanations are valid, yet the organization must continually examine possibilities for making interest rates to the poor as low as possible without jeopardizing its stated objectives.

An incarnational, contextual, empowering and sustainable methodology of mission

It has already been stated that Jesus is our role model for mission. This has particular application to the methodology of mission and, in particular, the development ministries that we are now reflecting on. Let us now examine four methodological principles.

1. Incarnational development

The impact of Jesus' ministry lies in the fact that "the Word became flesh and made his dwelling among us (John 1:14)," rather than a ministry delivered from a distance. For 30 years Jesus concentrated on *being* before he started *doing* anything. He intensely interacted with those to whom he ministered, including the women and the children whom society despised.

It is good to see the incarnational model so well represented in the cases before us. The Chidamoyo project is not content with just dispensing medicines for AIDS patient; it has adopted a model of caring through consoling, reconciling, loving and ministering. The patient and his or her family are thereby given a personal (incarnational) touch in all areas of their lives. The Food for the Hungry agricultural project also talks of the development worker being with the people, walking with them and seeking God's will in solving their problems. This is the incarnational approach at work. There is a sense of such an incarnational approach at work in other cases before us.

2. Contextual development

The incarnational approach naturally leads to a consideration of contextualization as a developmental method (for details see my thesis, "Contextualization of the Gospel in Zimbabwe"). All the ministries that Jesus carried out were in terms that recipients could understand and appropriate. His parables used what people saw and experienced in everyday life. When he fed the multitude he multiplied what they already had—the bread and the fish— and not the Italian pizza, which would have been strange to them. This is an example of contextualization.

The early church, too, started off in a Jewish context with a Jewish coloring. Circumcision continued to be practiced. Even Paul circumcised Timothy, whose mother was a Jew, so that their working together would not be a stumbling block to the Jews. Yet when the gospel spread to the Greco-Roman world it became similarly contextualized into the life and thought forms of the Gentiles. Indeed Paul, who is our best example of contextualization in the early church, wrote: "To the Jews I became like a Jew, to win the Jews. To those under the law I became like one under the law . . . so as to win those under the law. To those not having the law I became like one not having the law . . . so as to win those not having the law. To the weak I became weak, to win the weak. I have become all things to all men so that by all possible means I might save some (1 Corinthians 9:20-22)."

From the examples of Jesus and Paul we see that although the fundamental gospel is valid for all cultures and times, it must be clothed in time-bound cultural forms to be communicated and understood. Contextualization is the dynamic process whereby the constant message of the gospel interacts with specific, relative human situations. Although the gospel is unchanging, the contexts to which it relates are always changing. The gospel must relate to the whole context of humanity, both situational and experiential. The objective *situational* context(s) means all that is true of humanity in its given situation comprising the past, present and future; and a human being's lot in life including culture, nationality and laws. The gospel must also relate to the experiential context of humanity—the subjective experiences arising out of but also creating a human being's situational context, such as feelings of insecurity, hopes and fears. The totality of context is therefore very wide and forever changing. This makes contextualization an ongoing process wherever people preach and live out the gospel.

How, then, is contextualization reflected in the development ministries under review? Both of the AIDS projects give us an excellent example of a contextualized approach. The Uganda AIDS project case study states one of its critical assumptions: "Culturally adapted communications will result in a greater knowledge of God's Word and a better understanding of how to deal with AIDS, and music and drama are effective ways to communicate in this culture." The Chidamoyo home care program has adopted a contextualized approach through its program for AIDS patients, which utilizes family, community and church instead of the depersonalized, noncontextual and nonsustainable institutional approach.

Apart from the AIDS projects we note the thrust of contextualization in the Ansokia project, whose cornerstone is multidimensional, participatory, community-centered integrated development. The use of local, culturally appropriate resources in this project is highly commendable.

There is always a danger in development ministries of importing overseas methods and technologies that are alien and that create highly artificial and nonsustainable "development," which must perpetually depend on outside facilitators and resources to avoid crumbling. To this end I became concerned with the way the Luke Society uses high tech equipment like portable public address systems, recorded gospel messages and vehicles to transport people to crusades. Given the low level of development in this area, will this approach create in the recipients the impression that Christianity and a high level of technology are somehow synonymous? If the technology is withdrawn from this area, will Christianity still remain viable? This concern must be balanced against the consideration that there are situations where there are no effective alternatives to the use of such technologies.

3. Empowering development

The third methodological principle is that of empowerment. In simple terms this has to do with releasing the potential in recipients to enable them to continue helping themselves. This has often been explained in terms of the difference between continually giving a hungry man some fish (a relief or welfare approach), as opposed to teaching the man how to fish and then assisting him to acquire a hook and fishing line (development, empowerment). Of course if a man is already hungry it may be necessary to give him some fish first before he can learn the skill of fishing for himself.

As the children of Israel were in the wilderness for 40 years, God adopted a welfare approach, feeding them on manna and quail from heaven. The important thing, however, is that those same children of Israel were on the way to the Promised Land, where they could work with their own hands and not depend on handouts. Jesus fed the hungry in emergency situations, but he taught the value of hard work as the normative way. The most touching biblical story illustrating the welfare approach versus the empowering approach is that of the healing of the lame man who begged for money daily from those who entered the temple. Peter preferred the empowering approach: "In the name of Jesus Christ of Nazareth rise up and walk" (Acts 3:6 KJV). From that time that man would have the dignity of working for himself instead of being demeaned by handouts.

A very pleasing thing to note about the projects under review is the empowering approach taken. Zambuko Trust's holistic lending approach is an excellent example of empowerment in practice. It recognizes that many people have potential for self-employment where there is otherwise so much national unemployment. Zambuko does this by supplying the missing ingredients of loan capital and business skill to enable those without collateral security and who do not qualify for bank loans to run self-help businesses. And because empowerment is usually a gradual approach, Zambuko starts by lending small amounts and gradually increasing loans as the businesses grow and demonstrate their capacity to repay loans.

The empowering principle can also be seen in the number of projects that started with a relief approach and graduated to the empowering approach. This is well brought out in the example of the Rushinga cattle project, which passed through three phases—beginning with food distribution, proceeding to rehabilitation and then to development (the empowering approach). Other projects that have followed a similar path include the Ansokia program and World Vision Mozambique.

Empowerment presupposes a participatory mode of operation. Jesus often needed the people he helped to participate in the helping process in one way or the other. Sometimes participation came in the form of identifying their own needs, hence the question, "What do you want me to do for you?" Often the recipient was required to demonstrate a measure of faith. In the feeding miracles Jesus asked the people first to surrender what they already had. In the same way development programs must involve communities from the very beginning (needs identification, planning and implementation), recognizing that their motivation will be proportionate to their participation.

Our cases are replete with examples of participation. The Rushinga project utilized the participatory rural approach, and we can attribute the demonstrated success of this project in part to such grassroots participation.The Uganda AIDS project and the Ansokia program are among other projects that hold out the shining light of grassroots participation.

4. Sustainable development

We again revert to the example of Jesus in discussing the concept of sustainable development. His ministry lasted for only three years, yet the continuing impact of that ministry has just about covered the whole world. We can discern, in Jesus' approach, three main strategies for ensuring continuing sustainability: Jesus discipled his followers, trained the leaders, and entrusted the work to them. We can see this same threefold approach in the ministry of the apostle Paul. As we examine each of these we will compare them with the projects before us.

First, we note how Jesus discipled his followers. In Mark 3:14-15 we read, "He appointed twelve—designating them apostles—that they might be with him and that he might send them out to preach and to have authority to drive out demons." It is evident that the aspect of being "with him" would involve the development of a relationship with Jesus and would also be a time of being equipped with knowledge and skills. From the strength gained from the relationship and the skills imparted, the disciples would then be sent out for ministry. There is therefore a reproductive element involved in this process. Jesus was already reproducing skills in these men, enabling them to pass on the same skills to others. Paul articulates this process well: "And the things you have heard me say in the presence of many witnesses entrust to reliable men who will also be qualified to teach others" (2 Timothy 2:2). It is from such a scriptural base that the founder of the Navigators ministry, Dawson Trotman, declared to his followers, "Activity is no substitute for production, and production is no substitute for reproduction."

Often we hear of so-called development ministries where there is much activity and yet where there is nothing to show for the activity at the end of a given period. More often we see projects where there is indeed some production, and yet which fail when the outside facilitators have left. The missing ingredient in such "development" ministries is one of discipling people by genuinely imparting knowledge and skills that can be reproduced even when the outside facilitators have left.

Fortunately, in most of the projects under review there is consciousness of the need for a discipling process that can ensure continuity in those areas where discipling is happening. The participation mentioned above is a part of this discipling process. The Rushinga project promoted discipleship in the area of spiritual growth by dividing new believers into classes for a whole year of instruction. This followed a radical beginning of the lives of these new Christians when they burned the charms and other symbols of traditional worship.

In the Chidamoyo reproductive discipleship to AIDS patients, Ephraim and Juliet eventually led people into starting and leading a church in their home area. The Luke Society reports that committee members from previously planted churches are called upon to disciple new believers. Certainly such discipleship should lead to a change of lifestyle. For example in the Ansokia program it is reported that "dedicated Christianity brings good accountability. In various [program] committees, the Muslims and others are nominating the born-again Christians to be the treasurers of their flour mills, water development, revolving loan schemes and other committees." This is the sort of result we can expect from effective discipleship.

Second, we note that Jesus and Paul specifically trained leaders (reproducers) to a very high level of competence that would enable them to carry out ministry on their own. Although Jesus ministered to crowds, he spent more quality time with those who were going to lead. Paul ensured that people like Titus, Silas and Timothy understudied him to ensure that they could later be entrusted to undertake the work on their own. By the time Paul wrote his letters to Timothy and Titus, those two men were already leaders in charge of very difficult ministries in Crete and in Ephesus.

It has become common knowledge that in most development projects outside facilitators are happy enough to give generalized training (discipleship), but not high-level training that would equip a local leader to take over from the outside facilitator. The reason for such reluctance may lie in the fear of working oneself out of a job. The result is that after many years leadership of programs is still in the hands of outside facilitators, who seem to deliberately create inappropriate technologies and programs (with complicated reporting systems) that make it difficult for local leaders to take over. I would have wished to see good examples of high-level training of leadership for sustainable development in the projects under review. As the saying goes, there can be no success without a successor.

Last, we note how Jesus and Paul entrusted work to the equipped leaders as soon as possible. After three years of training his disciples Jesus issued the Great Commission: "Therefore go and make disciples of all nations . . ." (Matthew 28:19). These men were by no means perfect, but Jesus was willing to give them the privilege of making mistakes and learning from them. As for Paul, the most that he ever stayed at any one place during his missionary journeys was the three years that he spent at Ephesus. Yet we know that in his short stays at newly planted churches he was able to leave leaders whom he continued to encourage by letter and occasional visits.

I expect that a number of the projects represented here are practicing this aspect of entrusting work to trained leaders for the sake of long-term sustainability, although this has not been highlighted in the case studies.

Concluding remarks

I would like to thank the representatives of the various ministries for doing such a good job of articulating the nature and progress of their holistic work. This stimulated very helpful discussion at the consultation. All the participants went back enriched, equipped and encouraged to look again at what they are doing so that the good projects that are in progress can be made even better.

REFERENCES

Bosch, D. 1980. *Witness to the World*. Pretoria: New Foundation Theological Library.

Bosch, D. 1991. *Transforming Mission*. Maryknoll: Orbis Books.

Costas, O. E. 1974. *The Church and its Mission: A Shattering Critique from the Third World*. Wheaton: Tyndale House.

Escobar, S. and J. Driver. 1978. *Christian Mission and Social Justice*. Scottdale: Herald Press.

Musasiwa, R. 1990. "Contextualization of the Gospel in Zimbabwe." M.Th. thesis.

Padilla, C. R. 1985. *Mission Between the Times*. Grand Rapids: Eerdmans.

Stott, J. R. W. 1975. *Christian Mission in the World*. London: Falcon Books.

Yamamori, T., B. L. Myers and D. Conner, eds. 1995. *Serving with the Poor in Asia*. Monrovia: MARC.

Part three

Conclusion

14
At the end of the day

Bryant L. Myers

What can we say at the end of the day about holistic relief and development in Africa? What lessons can we draw from the eight case studies and the insightful comments from the perspectives of theology, anthropology and sociology, participation, management and missiology?

It is hard to say; relief and development is a difficult task and each experience is deeply enmeshed in a particular context and, hence, shaped by it. Comparing AIDS education and home care to emergency relief to cattle raising is a dangerous process indeed. Whatever I might say must be treated with care; it will not bear much weight.

I will group my reflections into three areas and deal with a series of questions in each of these areas.

Critical factors

- ❖ The importance of an incarnational approach
- ❖ The importance of quality ministry
- ❖ The importance of local culture
- ❖ The importance of holistic practitioners

Roles and relationships

- ❖ The role of the community

❖ The role of the church
❖ The role of donor agencies

Assessing the state of play

❖ What forms of Christian witness?
❖ What kinds of Christians are resulting from these experiences?
❖ What understanding of holistic ministry is appearing?

Critical factors in holistic ministry

The case studies and the reflection chapters point to four critical areas that appear central to continuing our learning as to what makes for and encourages holistic ministry that is genuinely transformational—spiritually and materially.

An incarnational approach. Over and over in the cases we learned of people going into the communities and often staying there. The cases suggest that getting close, sharing pain, working over the long term, making local commitments and loving people contributed significantly to the effectiveness of these ministries.

A cadre of trained relief and development professionals left the comforts of Addis Ababa to live among the poor in Ansokia. The Chidamoyo Christian Hospital in Zimbabwe switched its delivery strategy to making local believers and family members their arms and legs of compassion, because this was the only way to get close enough often enough to be effective. Living close to and praying with the dying AIDS patient proved a powerful witness in Zimbabwe and the AIDS awareness project in Uganda. Three Harare school leavers who were willing to relocate to distant Rushinga proved to be a critical factor in the success of the Rushinga cattle project.

As Roy Musasiwa compellingly points out in his chapter, this should not be surprising. Of all people, Christians should best understand the importance and effectiveness of an incarnational approach to helping others. The gospel is an encounter with a person, not merely a message. Life with Christ is just that. Even the two great commandments—loving God and loving our neighbor—

are relational in nature. Transformation is about relationships before it is about anything else.

Quality ministry. It is worthy of note that the quality of work was cited on several occasions as being important to people's showing interest in the gospel. The Kasei Clinic, the heartbeat of the Luke Society program in Ghana, points to its reputation for quality care as one of the factors that draws people to its work. This reputation extends to neighboring countries. The outstanding 97 percent loan repayment rate not only makes the Zambuko Trust in Zimbabwe a sustainable program but it is a powerful witness to the local banking and government circles that Christian work among the poor is worthy of emulation. People grow to trust such a program, and trusting Christian institutions is an important way to strengthen the witness of the churches. The Ansokia program cited development interventions that worked as a factor contributing to the attractiveness of the gospel.

Once again, we should not be surprised. When God created the cosmos, he declared that it was very good. Paul admonishes us to "work . . . with all your heart" (Colossians 3:23). God likes good work. We should strive to be every bit as professional as anyone else, and yet make it a professionalism with a difference.

The two sides of local culture. Local culture plays an interesting role in many of our cases. In some, local cultural beliefs and practices were a hindrance to development and were successfully challenged and transformed. In other cases, local culture proved to be an ally to the development process.

The Mozambique emergency relief project pointed to the factor of traditional beliefs intermingled with Christian faith as an inhibiting factor. The Mbarara agricultural project in Uganda reported that aversion to farming in preference to cattle raising was a hindrance to people adjusting to forced resettlement. The disruption of traditional authority structures by the resettlement was another obstacle. The AIDS home care project in Zimbabwe and the AIDS awareness project in Uganda pointed to the traditional religious beliefs concerning death and funerals as a major economic drain on the local people. The belief that illness was a result of witchcraft

215

meant expensive efforts with the local shaman to locate the person responsible for the curse. The Luke Society's case claims, "Traditional religious practices, which promote idolatry and demonic bondage, are one of the factors prohibiting prosperity and well-being within the country." In the Rushinga project, we heard the story of a local chief who had become a Christian, and his struggle to reconcile his new faith with his role as the mediator between his people and the spirit world. We learned that belief in fate and a negative attitude toward manual labor combined with an excessive number of religiously motivated non-work days served to undermine development in Ansokia.

At the same time, we also learned of local cultural practices that enhanced holistic ministry. The family and extended-family web of relationships and the traditions of sharing, even if one only had a little, were cited in both AIDS programs and the Luke Society work in Ghana. In Ansokia, the tradition of self-help local organizations was a development asset. Olivia Muchena points to the family and community structures, traditions of sharing and obligation, involvement and inclusivity and hunger for self-reliance as assets in African culture of which we must not fail to take advantage. She also reminds us that the integrated physical-spiritual world view of traditional cultures may provide the development practitioner with an important reminder of the limits of our modern world view and the technology derived from it.

We must remind ourselves that no culture is without blame or virtue. First, we must remind ourselves that the variety of cultures on God's earth is not a mistake God made. He created the world this way and we are told this is good. Therefore, we must celebrate the diversity and look for the fingerprints of God in every culture. Second, we must recognize that every culture is fallen and fails to reflect the goodness and justice of its Creator. The result of this tarnishing of culture is that every culture has elements that are not supportive of life and life abundantly. Such elements of culture must be transformed. In saying this, we must be careful not to succumb to the temptation of only recognizing the life-inhibiting or life-denying elements in the culture of the other; they lie in our culture as well.

Holistic ministry that is truly biblical must point to the anti-gospel elements of the holistic practitioner and even the funding agency as well as pointing to such elements in traditional communities.

Holistic practitioners. The effectiveness of holistic ministry always comes down to the character, qualities and skills of those who carry it out. The cases repeatedly point to this. The Mozambique emergency relief project is the story of people who went to dangerous places, lived hard lives and somehow managed to handle a rapidly growing program at the same time that they taught in churches and witnessed after hours. The Rushinga project tells of a pastor and his wife, comfortable in Harare, accepting God's challenge to work past "where the tar road ends." The pastor's "evangelism first" approach was turned around by his experience among Mozambican refugees. The Luke Society project began because a physician moved to a medical clinic in a five room house with no electricity where he created a program of heath care, income generation, evangelism and collaborative links with every other resource God had put in his area of work.

If transformation is the product of relationships, then the formation of the holistic practitioner is the critical factor. Our consultation gives us some important pointers in this regard. The experience of the Rushinga project led the denomination to add a development course to their Bible school and to change their evangelism strategy. Olivia Muchena calls for the use of indigenous knowledge systems as a better point of departure for our development journey with the people. Samuel Voorhies points to the importance of training in the skills of facilitation and community organization as keys to effective local participation. Kwame Bediako insists that a Christian response to the poor is invariably a theological response, yet we seldom insist on theological training for development practitioners nor do we add theological reflection to the development planning or evaluation process. Finally, Kweku Hutchful makes a powerful case for a genuinely Christian understanding of management as it is applied to the development process. Too often what management training we provide to holistic practitioners is straight off the shelves of the modern management supermarket, and this leads to a practice that perhaps is more professional, but is not always Christian. As Hutchful roots his understanding of management in the creation account, he creates some very interesting parallels with the same theology that undergirds our understanding of holistic ministry to the poor.

Roles and relationships

I have posited that relationship is critical to any transformative process. I would like to call attention to some issues concerning relationships that arise from our cases.

The role of the community. The community must be the subject of its own development. The holistic practitioner accompanies this process; the Spirit of God initiates and sustains it. Our cases point repeatedly to the importance of community participation that is genuine and sustained, and they also call attention to the tangible contribution communities can make to the resourcing of the programs. Voorhies makes a powerful case for this in his chapter.

The Luke Society project affirms that the "involvement of the local community members is a crucial part in the founding of these clinics. . . . They donate the land for the clinic and help build the clinic structure." The Mbarara agricultural project in Uganda reports that, "Although the government representative of the area at first said the people were unable to manage any kind of project themselves, the people have now organized their own school and community development committees to discuss improvements . . ." In the Rushinga project, community leaders now run the entire program, with outside assistance limited to writing funding proposals.

We also learned that mobilization of local resources was a critical element in developing local ownership and avoiding dependency relationships. This was cited in the case of Ansokia as a key to sustainability. The Rushinga project reports that improving the livelihoods of the local people led to strong church support, and the daughter churches are now providing support to the mother church in Harare. The Zambuko Trust project was organized because someone had faith that local people could some day support growing local churches.

If we can affirm that God has always been at work in the communities where we work, then we must also affirm that the table is already set. Our arrival is no surprise to God. We simply need the eyes to see and the ears to hear. Resources and gifts are already there. The potential for local ownership and participation is always present.

The role of the church. It is hard to miss the fact that every one of our cases is the result of the activity of what some call parachurch agencies. For a long time, the debate has gone on as to how the holistic ministry to which some specialty Christian agencies have been called relates to the local church in the community and the institutional church in the country. In his chapter, Roy Musasiwa makes a strong case for the church as the primary agent of God's mission. He calls for holistic ministries to be closely related to the work of the church. What is interesting is that our cases seem to be aware of this fact and speak to this issue in some interesting ways. They go beyond simply involving the church to strengthening the church.

The Uganda AIDS awareness project is very clear in its intent to strengthen the church: "The local church was involved in the program from its inception. . . . A primary goal is to use and build on existing church structures and institutions, primarily through training. . . . The church is the primary implementer . . ." In the Mbarara agricultural project the farmers are encouraged to share their produce with the church, and church leaders have been encouraged to respond by making personal visits to the farmers. "This has improved the sense of community and increased church involvement." The AIDS home care project team "quickly decided that the best people to involve in caring for the AIDS patients and their families were local Christians," and turned to the local Church of Christ churches. Both the Zambuko Trust and Rushinga projects show clear evidence that increased economic well-being has also resulted in increased support to local churches. The Ansokia project was started where there was no church and, as new believers emerged, called an existing church to take over responsibility for the new believers. The Mozambique emergency relief project put a major church training and equipping program in place, although it admits that it might have done more to integrate this effort with the churches in the locality where its food distribution, health services and agricultural recovery work was taking place.

It seems that parachurch agencies may be breaking some new ground. Desiring that their work strengthen the local church and make it more attractive in the eyes of the community is important, but there may be a further discovery on the horizon. Is it possible that the agencies God has set aside to do Christian relief and development may begin to accept and believe the discovery of the Ansokia project? "The experience of Ansokia I ADP shows that the existence of a dynamic and growing church and Christian community is an indispensable factor for sustainable transformational development."

Donor agencies. Some of the cases introduced an interesting, and sometimes disturbing, note regarding the role of donor agencies. In several of the cases, funding from Western governments has resulted in a struggle on the part of the Christian relief and development agency to find ways around the restrictions such funding places on "religious or spiritual" activities. This was mentioned in the Zambuko Trust case study and was cited as a major problem in the Mozambique emergency relief effort. I think it is important to note that this is a Western problem. The AIDS home care case from Zimbabwe made a point of saying that the Zimbabwe government did not place any restrictions and, in fact, encouraged the spiritual nature of their work. Muchena raises eloquent concern and correctly locates this as a question as to which shrine we choose to worship. Bediako asks "how far they [Christian agencies] can go in concealing their religious convictions regarding social questions in initial contacts with secular funding agencies." I think we need to do more than that. We need to tackle the underlying issue head-on.

A dialogue has been going on in Canada for the past four years between the religious NGOs and the Canadian government on this very issue. The religious NGOs have challenged the Canadian International Development Agency (CIDA) on their practice of forbidding religious and spiritual activities in CIDA-funded projects in the Third World. The religious NGOs have asked on what grounds CIDA makes this prohibition in light of the fact that the communities where the projects were carried out have a seamless physical-spiritual world view. Wasn't the CIDA restriction nothing more than the imposition of a Western secular world view on Third World communities? Wasn't this simply another expression of post-colonial behavior? After much hemming and hawing, CIDA acknowledged the truth of this claim, and the door was finally opened to the important underlying question: What is the role of religion in the process of human and social transformation? I wonder if this kind of challenge does not need to find a voice throughout the Christian relief and development community and the church in the Two-Thirds World. By accepting restrictions of this kind without protest, are we not in fact the true source of power by which this imposition take place? Challenging these odious assumptions may be the only way to create the space for change.

Assessing the state of play

As we examine the cases, it is tempting to say a few things about the state of play of the Christian relief and development agencies. The sample represented by the cases is far too small for anything definite to be said, but a few questions might stimulate useful reflection in the future.

What forms of Christian witness? Each of the case writers was asked to describe "the process of people coming to know Christ." The answers varied somewhat, but some themes are clear.

Personal, loving Christians is a factor that we cannot overstate. The Ansokia case pointed to the "exemplary lives of the staff" and what "staff did in saving people from physical death, in nursing the sick and in helping to bury the dead." The two AIDS project cases made it clear that accompanying people who were rejected by others through death creates a powerful witness. The "Rushinga approach" of assessing needs first and then doing evangelism has now become a model in many program locations, and points to a personal, people-centered approach. My earlier statements about the importance of incarnation are reinforced by these experiences.

Partnership with churches committed to outreach was another theme. The Uganda agricultural project spoke of personal visits by church leaders, the Jesus film and a partnership with Life Ministries, a Ugandan evangelistic ministry. The Zambuko Trust pointed to the critical role of the local church doing what the trust could not do without the danger of creating "credit" Christians. The Luke Society added prayer and fasting as the undergirding tools for Christian witness, and also pointed to the importance of deliverance ministries in deeply spiritual Africa.

In every case, the people were given the opportunity to hear the claims of the gospel and an opportunity to respond. The good deeds of the gospel were always accompanied by good words.

What kinds of Christians? It was interesting to note the way the new believers were described in the cases. In the Rushinga project, new believers burned their charms in declaration of their freedom in Christ from the spirits, and they also began to share their new wealth with the church. The Zambuko Trust spends a lot of time working on Christian values in the marketplace, promoting stewardship and avoiding tempting people to become Christians in order to receive loans. The AIDS home care project spoke of people changing lifestyles, of ethical behavior alongside personal piety and of traditional practices such as inheritance of the widow by the brother. The Ansokia story called attention to churches now involved in sustaining the development process. The "evangelistic results" were not generally reported in terms of numbers. There is a sense that a kind of holistic Christian may be resulting from this holistic process.

This is important progress. Too often the "evangelism first" (and usually only) approach results in people with saved souls and unchanged social lives. A purely spiritual message implies that becoming and then being a Christian is a purely spiritual transition. The tendency is for new believers to go to church and practice personal piety, but withdraw from the world from which they came into the safe and welcoming arms of the church, never to return. Bediako correctly worries about "a gospel that focuses on numbers of believers, rather than on the depth of sociocultural and religious impact."

The stories from our cases are mixed. School leaver converts went to a poor area of the country to work in a cattle project and witness to their faith. Would-be pastors receive development training. Social practices change in ways that undergird the possibility of a better future in material terms. Other stories sound like personal faith and personal lifestyle changes. In no case did we see evidence of significant engagement with social and political structures, even when it was clear that they were part of the problem. We are clearly still in process in understanding how holistic ministry creates genuinely holistic practitioners.

What understanding of holistic ministry is appearing? One final reflection: We need to keep asking the question about what we mean by holistic ministry. This is important because we are aware that our understanding of holistic ministry is not all it might be. Our understanding of holistic ministry is infected with the modern world view, which separates the physical from the spiritual. In this framework, evangelism is understood as a spiritual activity and discipleship is reduced to the care and feeding of the redeemed soul. Christianity becomes a personal, internal religious experience exercised in public on Sunday mornings. The messy, unjust and painful material world is seemingly left to the Devil, and social action—relief, development, working for justice or caring for the environment—is somewhat suspect as legitimate Christian work. This is the underlying philosophical cause of the long-standing debate about the primacy of evangelism and the second class status of social action as a Christian ministry. Musasiwa's comments on the world of humanity being the object of God's mission speaks to this.

Christian relief and development agencies represent the first steps in a corrective against this mindset, and it is not easy. The Zambuko Trust case speaks poignantly of the resistance it receives from church leaders for pursuing a ministry that is not deemed fully Christian. The fact that this view comes from Western church leaders affirms the thesis that a Western view of modernity is influencing the Western church's understanding of mission.

Our cases reveal a significant level of integration of activities. Health, agriculture, pastoral care for the dying, relief, income generation, cattle raising, revolving loans of money and cattle, evange-lism, prayer and fasting—all find their expressions in our cases. This is good news, and we should celebrate our progress.

Bediako, however, speaks a prophetic word and pushes us another important step. Integration is not the same as organic unity. Putting pieces of a living thing back in their proper place is integra-tion, but it does not mean there is life. Life is sustained and possible only if we do not take the living thing apart in the first place. Our cases reveal integration, but not so much the living, interacting wholeness that I suspect the living Word promises for the living gospel of the living Lord.

If transformation finds its expression in relationships, then holism is and must be in the practitioner. Certainly it was the per-son Jesus in whom we find our model for holism, not in a particu-lar set of activities he did. The fundamental transformative relationship is with God through Jesus Christ, and we will only experience transformation toward the kingdom values of commu-nity and sharing, justice and peace, productive work and creation of wealth as our relationships with each other and our environment are transformed by the work of Christ's disciples. Bediako reminds us, "Just as the gospel is a person not a program, so holistic min-istry must be personal, not programmatic." We are making progress and we still have a long way to go.

Muchena adds another piece to our struggle for a better under-standing of holism: "For ministry to be truly holistic, it must be seen as holistic by the person receiving the ministry and not just by the person providing it." We might learn a great deal about holism if we were willing to allow those we serve to tell us how we are doing. How many of us go to the communities and declare what we hope and dream in terms of a better human future, and then ask them how we are doing? Since most Africans have never had the problem of a two-tiered, physical-spiritual world view, we might be surprised about how much we might learn about our own mod-ern biases.

Part four

Appendixes

Appendix A:
Consultation participants

Some 30 practitioners, theorists and representatives gathered in Harare, Zimbabwe, in November 1995 to discuss effective holistic ministry in Africa. Following is a list of participants, their affiliations and the countries in which they are based.

Name	Organization	Country
Kwame Bediako	Akrofi-Christaller Memorial Center	Ghana
John Boateng	The Luke Society	Ghana
David Bussau	Opportunity Foundation	Australia
Paul Dell	Springs Ministries	South Africa
Phineas Dube	Central Baptist Church	Zimbabwe
Steve Ferguson	Fieldstead Institute	U.S.A.
Beyene Gutema	World Vision	Ethiopia
Cristina Houtz	Fieldstead Institute	U.S.A.
Kweku Hutchful	Leaders International	Zimbabwe
Gary Kusunoki	Calvary Chapel	U.S.A.
Cheryl Lovejoy	Opportunity International	Zimbabwe
Hyeong Lyeol Lyu	Food for the Hungry	Uganda
E. Maphenduka	Zambuko Trust	Zimbabwe
Michael Mbito	African Evangelistic Enterprise	Kenya
Kathy McCarty	Chidamoyo Christian Hospital	Zimbabwe
Major Mereki	Chidamoyo Christian Hospital	Zimbabwe
Olivia Muchena	World Vision	Zimbabwe
Roy Musasiwa	Domboshowa House Theological College	Zimbabwe

Name	Organization	Country
Denias B. Musona	United Baptist Church	Zimbabwe
P. Nyatsambo	Zambuko Trust	Zimbabwe
Gregory Rake	MAP International	U.S.A.
Larry Reed	Opportunity International	Zimbabwe
Don and Diana Schmierer	Fieldstead Institute	U.S.A.
J. R. Shenk	Brethren in Christ Church	Zimbabwe
Mary Tyler	Food for the Hungry	Uganda
Tomas Valoi	World Vision	Mozambique
Samuel Voorhies	World Vision	Zimbabwe
Christopher Wachepa	Prison Fellowship	Zambia
Ted Yamamori	Food for the Hungry	U.S.A.

Appendix B:
Case study guidelines

Holistic ministry practitioners attending the November 1995 consultation in Harare, Zimbabwe, wrote case studies of effective holistic ministry in Africa. The authors used the following five guidelines.

1. Acquaint yourself with the concept of holistic ministry.

Although reconciliation with others is not reconciliation with God, nor is social action evangelism, nor is political liberation salvation, nevertheless we affirm that evangelism and sociopolitical involvement are both part of our Christian duty.

Both are necessary expressions of our doctrines of God and man, our love for our neighbor and our obedience to Jesus Christ (see section five of the Lausanne Covenant). Tetsunao Yamamori expresses this concept as follows:

> Ministering to physical needs and ministering to spiritual needs, though functionally separate, are relationally inseparable, and both are essential to the total ministry of Christ's church.

2. Provide the context of your case study.

Describe the people group with whom you have done your work. What is their history as a people group? In what material and spiritual ways were they poor? What were their economic, social, political and religious circumstances? What were their religious beliefs when you started?

3. Describe your holistic ministry program.

What type of development project did you implement (water, food production, health, microenterprise, integrated development)? Describe it in some detail. How did it come into being? What kind of development process did you use? How was or were the church(es) involved? How was Christian witness to take place?

4. What were the results?

What kind of material or physical transformation has taken place? How have the lives of the poor improved? What evidence of spiritual transformation in people and in the community have you seen? What evidence of cultural or social transformation have you seen?

5. Describe the process of people coming to know Christ.

What happened here? As a result of lifestyle evangelism of some individual staff members? As a result of a specific evangelistic strategy of your organization? As a result of your partnership with a local church?

Were there dynamic individuals who played a key role in bringing people to Christ? Give details. How many people accepted Christ? Who actually came to accept Christ? As individuals, families, or as villagers together?

6. Identify the factors which contributed to the emergence of a Christ group (a growing church or a new group of believers).

Why did people come to know Christ through the development project in which you were engaged? Were there any specific decisions made by individuals or your organization which resulted in the conversion of people? What was your own part in the result of the case?

7. Evaluate your case study.

Looking at the case, are there things you would or should have done to improve the result? What do you think were some obstacles which retarded the progress of the spiritual ministry?